Stimulating
Simulations

Second Edition

The Hayden Microcomputer Series

Consulting Editor: Ted Lewis, Oregon State University

†Consulting Editor: Sol Libes, Amateur Computer Group of New Jersey and
  Union Technical Institute

Stimulating
Simulations

Second Edition

C. W. Engel

HAYDEN BOOK COMPANY, INC.
Rochelle Park, New Jersey

ISBN 0-8104-5170-0
Library of Congress Catalog Card Number 79-88327

6 7 8 9   PRINTING
82 83 84 85 86 87   YEAR

Contents

Stimulating Simulations

Second Edition

INTRODUCTION

Simple number games and puzzles are frequently developed by beginning computer hobbyists. While some enthusiasts develop computer systems that monitor environmental conditions, compute income tax, or serve as expensive burglar alarms, most continue to use their computers primarily for recreation. This book is designed for the person who is beyond the simple number-game stage of software development and would like to develop some interesting simulations. It is assumed that the reader is familiar with most of the BASIC commands and has written some simple programs.

Most of the programs in this book are written so that the computer does not do all of the "thinking" but forces the player to develop strategies for achieving the objectives. A general overview of a simulation is illustrated in the flowchart below.

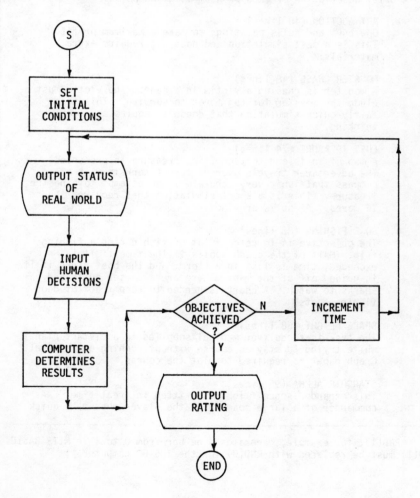

The simulations presented in this book are written in BASIC and can be easily adapted to almost any system.* The programs vary from 500 to 2,000 bytes or 32 to 115 lines of BASIC. Some of the lines have multiple statements; but, since the line numbers are multiples of ten, it would be easy to modify the programs to operate with single statements.

Each simulation begins with a scenario describing the rules, conditions and objectives to be achieved. The rules have been written in second person, because some programmers like to condense the rules and place them in a subroutine for access by the operator. A sample run and a general flowchart with line numbers provide additional information about each program. A description of the variables precedes the program listing. Some program modifications are suggested. The minor modifications require only adjustments of variables in specific lines, while major modifications require additional programming. In some cases, supplemental playing boards, graphs, and charts are supplied for recording information on the progress of the simulation.

A brief description of each program is given below.

1. ART AUCTION (48 lines)
    One buys and sells paintings to make a maximum profit.
    This is a fast simulation and does not require extra
    materials.

2. MONSTER CHASE (48 lines)
    A monster is chasing a victim in a cage. The victim must
    elude the monster for ten moves to survive. This is a
    fairly quick simulation that doesn't require too much
    thinking.

3. LOST TREASURE (74 lines)
    A map of an island that contains treasure is presented.
    The adventurer travels over different terrain with a
    compass that isn't very accurate in an attempt to find the
    treasure. This is a short simulation that requires about
    15 moves. A map is provided.

4. GONE FISHING (83 lines)
    The objective is to catch a lot of fish during a fishing
    trip. Half of the catch spoils if the time limit is
    exceeded, time is lost in a storm, and the boat sinks if it
    is guided off of the map. There are also sea gulls and
    sharks to watch. A chart is needed to keep track of good
    fishing spots.

5. SPACE FLIGHT (68 lines)
    The task is to deliver medical supplies to a distant planet
    while trying to stay on course without running out of fuel.
    Graph paper is required to plot the course.

6. STARSHIP ALPHA (98 lines)
    This expanded space flight is written in "real time." As
    commander of a large spaceship, the player must make quick,

---

*RND(1), for example, generates a number from 0 to 1 in MITS BASIC.
RND(1) must be replaced with RND(0) for the TRS-80 computer.

logical decisions regarding landing instructions, crew
morale, the black hole, radiation, aliens, and the use of
shields, gyros and lazer beams.

7. FOREST FIRE (77 lines)
    The objective is to subdue a forest fire with chemicals and
    backfires. The success of a firefighter is based on the
    time needed to control the fire and to completely
    extinguish it.

8. NAUTICAL NAVIGATION (70 lines)
    This simulation requires the navigation of a sailboat to
    three different islands, using a radio direction finder.
    The wind direction is an important variable. Graph paper,
    protractor and ruler are needed to plot the course.

9. BUSINESS MANAGEMENT (92 lines)
    In this simulation, raw materials are bought and finished
    products are produced and sold. The cost of materials and
    production and the selling price vary each month. The
    objective is to maximize the profits. No extra materials
    are required.

10. RARE BIRDS (75 lines)
    This is a bird watching simulation. The objective is to
    identify as many different birds as possible. A record of
    those identified is helpful and a bird watching chart is
    provided.

11. DIAMOND THIEF (83 lines)
    One assumes the role of a detective is this simulation. A
    thief has just stolen a diamond from a museum. Five suspects
    must be questioned to determine the thief. A floor plan of
    the museum and a chart indicating suspects and times are
    provided.

12. THE DEVIL'S DUNGEON (115 lines)
    A fantasy adventure into a bottomless cave. The player
    must chart his way, fight monsters, poisonous gas and
    demons to escape with the gold.

The SOCCER program developed in the last section of the Introduction
is designed for two players, although it could be modified so that the
computer is one of the players. In this simulation, each player controls
a team of five soccer players whose objective is to kick the ball across
the opponent's goal line. This program is written in three stages to
illustrate the procedure for modifying and expanding already existing
simulations.

In addition to extending the simulations in this book, the reader
might try combining some of them. For example, one could use the money
earned in Art Auction to start the Business Management simulation. After
twelve months of business, the profits could be used to buy a boat to use
in the Gone Fishing simulation. A larger boat could survive more storms,
hold more fish, and allow fishing in deeper water. The ultimate
objective could be to catch the most fish.

The computer hobbyist is limited only by the imagination in
simulating real events. It is the author's desire that this book provide
some fun and, at the same time, stimulate further development of creative

simulations. Some additional ideas for simulations are suggested below.

1. Hunt Big Foot
2. Race a Sailboat
3. Inhibit the Andromeda Strain
4. Stop the African Bee Invasion
5. Climb Mountains
6. Survive in the Wilderness
7. Find Gold or Oil
8. Swim from Sharks
9. Dispatch Airplanes, Trains, or Trucks
10. Herd Sheep
11. Explore Caves
12. Catch Butterflys

The next section offers some guidelines for developing simulation activities.

DEVELOPING SIMULATIONS

A Creative Process

If one has a mathematical problem for computer solution, the programming process can be approached in the following manner: 1) Develop the flowchart. 2) Define the variables. 3) Write the initial program. 4) Debug. 5) Run. In developing a simulation activity, however, there is a great deal more creative effort involved; and the steps listed above are not necessarily implemented in sequence. One can compare the development of a simulation program to that of a creative artist such as a painter. The blank computer memory is the canvas and BASIC language represents the paint and brushes. An artist continually retouches and reworks the painting until the final product meets the artist's criteria for success.

Most technological advances, such as television and radio, are "one-way streets" -- one observes what takes place. The observer seldom creates, composes or interacts with such devices. Developing simulation programs for computers can provide intelligent people with an opportunity to react with their environment in a problem-solving mode.

Selecting a Topic

The first task in developing a computer simulation is to select a topic. Almost any idea could serve as a starting point; however, the reader's own interests and hobbies are usually the best resource for ideas. The possibilities are unlimited. One could develop simulations on cooking, stamp collecting, gardening, racing cars, dating, jogging or dreaming. With a little research, a long-desired ambition could become material for an exciting simulation -- a safari across Africa, a trip around the world, or a walk on the moon. The creative programmer can be transported to any time or any place in the universe via the computer simulation.

Once a topic for the simulation is selected, the next step is to write down a fairly detailed description of what the program will accomplish. This narration will become the scenario. To illustrate this process, the author has chosen "survival in a jungle" as a topic.

Jungle Survival Scenario

You have crashed somewhere in the middle of an uninhabited jungle island in the Pacific. You will have to select a limited quantity from the provisions on the plane. The more provisions you carry, the slower you will travel. As you travel across the island, you will encounter various hazards with which you must deal. The terrain will consist of mountains, rivers, plains, swamps and lakes. Crossing a mountain range will be slow, but it will provide a more direct route. Traveling down a river will be easy, but a variety of unpredictable hazards will occur. Your objective is to hike to the perimeter of the island in as few days as possible.

The scenario should provide answers to the following questions.

1. What will the operator do?
2. What feedback will the computer provide?
3. What surprise elements will produce fun and excitement?
4. What are the winning conditions?
5. How will the success of the simulation be measured?

The writer must realize that the first scenario is only an approximation to the final product. As the program is developed and field tested, the scenario will probably change considerably.

While developing the scenario, the writer should begin to visualize a sample run. In the case of the jungle survival program, a sample run might look something like the following.

```
CHOOSE YOUR PROVISIONS:  1  FOOD
                         2  WATER
                         .
                         .
                         N  XXXXXXX

READY TO START JOURNEY?
YOU ARE AT POSITION 42,43.  IN THE CLEAR
CHOOSE THE DIRECTION OF YOUR NEXT MOVE?  N
HOW FAR WOULD YOU LIKE TO GO?  32 MILES

YOU ARE AT POSITION 42,42.  IN THE MOUNTAINS
CHOOSE THE DIRECTION OF YOUR NEXT MOVE?  E
HOW FAR WOULD YOU LIKE TO GO?  10 MILES

YOU FELL INTO THE RIVER!
```

The sample run listed above has several problems. First, the distance the player can travel in a given time-interval should be limited. Also, one should probably be able to see mountains ahead. At this point in the development of the program, however, the writer should have decided that the output of the computer will include the location of the player, the type of terrain, and a request for the player to select the direction of travel.

Flowchart

The next step in developing a simulation is to construct a general flowchart. In the case of the jungle survival simulation, the first flowchart might take the following form.

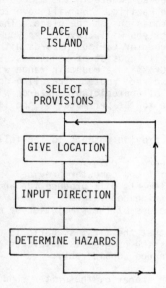

It is not necessary to provide all of the details in the flowchart in the beginning. It is better to start writing the program and develop the flowchart along with the program. The flowchart should provide a graphic aid to the programming and need only be developed to the extent that the programmer feels it is necessary to keep track of the flow of ideas.

Selecting the Variables

It is a good idea to keep a list of the variables used in the program. If such a list is not referred to and continually updated, the same variable might be used to represent two different things. Usually the letters, I, J, K, are used for indexing loops; and the first one or two letters of a word are selected for major variables in the program, e.g., T for time. It is also useful to designate a range for the variables.

In the jungle survival program, a list of the variables might be as follows.

		Range
X,Y	position on island	0 - 100
T	time on island	0 - 100
E	energy of survivor	0 - 100
W	weight of provisions	0 - 50
MX,MY	location of mountains	
LX,LY	location of lakes	

```
CX.CY      location of clearings
M          direction of movement
```

The list of variables should be expanded as needed during the writing of the program.

Subroutines

One of the reasons given for using subroutines is to limit the amount of repetition in a program. Another use of subroutines is to provide flexibility in developing a program. The main parts of a program can be written first and subroutines can be used to add the details later. The use of subroutines frees the writer from having to determine in advance how many lines are needed between main parts of the program. Also, the main parts of the program can be more easily identified if subroutines are used to handle the details.

The use of subroutines, as described above, is illustrated below.

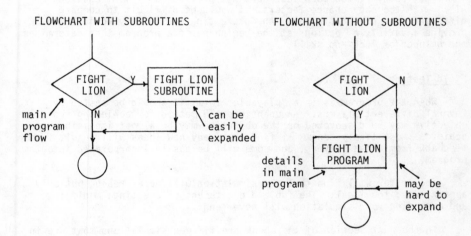

Writing the Program

After developing a rough flowchart, one can start to write and test the first part of the program. It is not usually a good idea to type in and test a long, complicated program in its entirety. The writer should make sure that the first part of the program works independently. Usually after some experimentation with the initial part of the program, one will think of new ideas; and the flowchart and/or scenario will be revised. The programmer should not forget to keep an updated version of the program on a disk or tape to avoid a second typing of the program due to an accidental loss of memory.

Sometimes the writer may find a particular objective very difficult to program. Rather than spend considerable time trying to achieve what may be impossible, it would be advisable to change the scenario. Quite often such "open-mindedness" leads to a more interesting or more elegant simulation than was originally anticipated. The writer, on the other hand, should not hesitate to program what might seem like a complex idea. Many times complex ideas are easy to program, while simple ideas are very difficult to program. The programmer should not strive for perfection. Most programs could probably be "neater" or more elegant with the invest- ment of a few more hours of programming time; however, the only accomplishment might be to save a few milliseconds during the run.

The simulation should be fairly simple at first, until it is running. Then the programmer can add the "bells and whistles" if desirable. Sometimes too much complexity distracts from the enjoyment of the simulation, especially if it takes another computer to operate the simulation.

When writing a program, one should keep all program statements involving a similar idea together. Such a practice will make debugging a program much easier. A brief summary of the instructions for the simulation is also worthwhile if memory capacity is sufficient.

It is sometimes difficult to provide an appropriate balance between skill and luck. The chance factors provide interest, excitement and intrigue; however, too much luck does not provide sufficient challenge. Also, with too many chance factors, it would be difficult to compare different runs of the program. An interesting possibility would be to provide a variety of options at the beginning of a program that determines the balance of luck and skill.

Field Testing

When the program is in a "playable" form, it should be tested by several different players. An unanticipated method for achieving the objective may be discovered or the objective may be almost impossible to achieve. Most likely, one will find that many new ideas will result from feedback from these players, and some will be easily incorporated into the program.

The writer will find that the simulation will never reach, but only approximate, the ideal. The fun and excitement of creating, modifying, and expanding your simulation will never end.

In the next section of this book are fifteen simulations that are in a playable form; however, they are only the beginning for the person with a creative mind.

MODIFYING AND EXPANDING SIMULATIONS

Each program in this book concludes with a list of suggested modifications. This section illustrates how to modify and expand a simple program, SOCCER I, to the more sophisticated SOCCER II and SOCCER III. These three programs require two people to operate the computer, where each person controls five players on a playing field.

The objective in SOCCER I is to eliminate the opponent's players. SOCCER I is the least sophisticated of the three programs and does not provide for incorrect inputs from the keyboard.

In SOCCER II, the objective is to be the first team to pick up a ball that is resting in the middle of the field. Sidelines are drawn in this program, and a player's movement can be stopped by pressing the space bar. Incorrect key entries are ignored.

In the last version presented here, SOCCER III, one must kick the ball across the opponent's goal line. When a player touches the ball, it moves in one of three random directions toward the goal, unless it is blocked by an opponent. Injured players appear on the sidelines.

The technique of modifying and/or expanding existing programs is very valuable. It would be a good exercise for the student to continue expanding this program by using the suggestions listed at the end of the SOCCER III section.

SOCCER I

Scenario

This simulation requires two people to play. One person controls the five letters, A, B, C, D and E; another person controls the five numerals, 1, 2, 3, 4 and 5. In the beginning, the letters appear on the left side of the screen and the numerals appear on the right side of the screen. A small dot will appear on either the left or right side of the screen to indicate which player can take a turn.

A turn consists of moving one of the five players by entering the appropriate numeral or letter, followed by an arrow entry to indicate the general direction of movement. A player moves ten spaces each turn. If a player lands on an opponent, the game is over. Incorrect key entries must be avoided in this program or the program will halt.

Sample Run

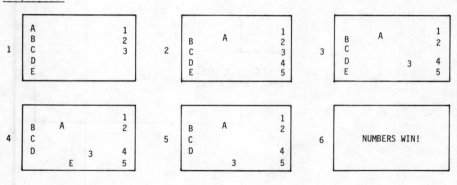

SOCCER I FLOWCHART

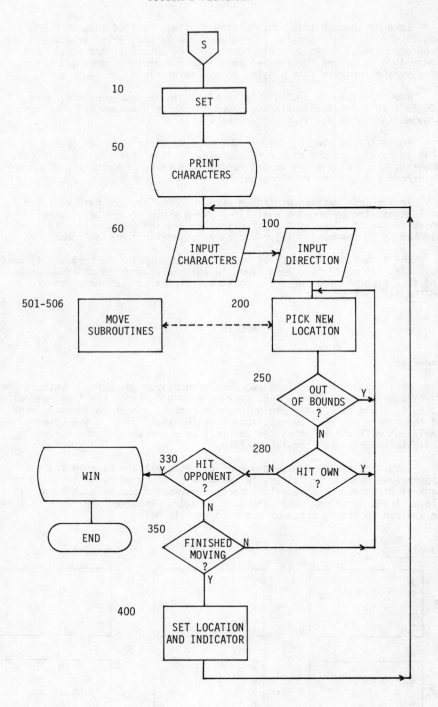

SOCCER I PROGRAM

Variables

I,J,K	Indices
P	Player
L(I)	Location of player
X$	Input character
N	ASCII code of character
Y$	Input direction
D	ASCII code of direction
L	Old location
M	New location
E,F	Temporary variables

Program Listing

```
  5   REM SET
 10   DEFINT I-W:DEFSTR X-Z:CLS:P=1:RESTORE
 20   FOR I=1 TO 10:READ L(I):NEXT
 30   DATA 198,326,454,582,710,249,377,505,633,761

 35   REM PRINT
 50   FOR I=1TO5:PRINT@L(I),CHR$(64+I);:NEXT:FOR I=6TO10:PRINT@L(I),
      CHR$(43+I);:NEXT:SET(0,47)

 55   REM INPUT
 60   X=INKEY$:IF X=""THEN 60:REM NO SPACE
 70   N=ASC(X)
 80   IF P=1 THEN N=N-64 ELSE N=N-43
 90   L=L(N)
100   Y=INKEY$:IF Y=""THEN 100
110   D=ASC(Y)

195   REM START MOVE
200   FOR I=1 TO 10
210   IF D=10 THEN M=L+58+3*RND(3)
220   IF D=91 THEN M=L-58-3*RND(3)
230   IF D=9 THEN ON RND(3) GOSUB 501,502,503
240   IF D=8 THEN ON RND(3) GOSUB504,505,506
250   E=(M-3)/64:F=(M+4)/64
260   IF M<64 OR M>895 THEN M=L:GOTO350
270   IF INT(E)-E=0 OR INT(F)-F=0 THEN M=L:GOTO350

275   REM CHECKS
280   FOR K=1 TO 10
290   IF K=N THEN 340
300   IF M<>L(K) THEN340
310   IF P=1 AND K<6 THEN M=L:GOTO 340
320   IF P=2 AND K>5 THEN M=L:GOTO 340
330   CLS:IF P=1 PRINT@410,"LETTERS WIN!";ELSE PRINT@410,
      "NUMBERS WIN!";
335   FOR I=1 TO 1000:NEXT J:RUN
340   NEXT K:PRINT@L," ";:L=M:PRINT@M,X;
350   NEXT I

395   REM FINISH MOVE
400   L(N)=M
```

```
410    IF P=1 THEN P=2 ELSE P=1
420    IF P=1 THEN SET(Ø,47):RESET(127,47)
430    IF P=2 THEN SET(127,47):RESET(Ø,47)
450    GOTO6Ø
501    M=L+3:RETURN
502    M=L-61:RETURN
503    M=L+67:RETURN
504    M=L-3:RETURN
505    M=L+61:RETURN
506    M=L-67:RETURN
```

Soccer II

This program is an extension of the previous program, SOCCER I. It is a good idea to have SOCCER I running before proceeding with the modifications and additions suggested in this section.

Scenario

In this simulation, as in SOCCER I, two people control five players each. The major difference is the objective -- to be the first to land on a ball resting in the middle of the field. You can eliminate more than one of your opponent's players. Also, you can stop your own player's movement by pressing the space bar.

A border is drawn around the field, and prompts are printed at the bottom of the field to indicate each player's turn and the character that has been entered. Inappropriate entries from the keyboard are not accepted. The strength of the players, which diminishes with each move and increases when resting, determines the players' ability to move and eliminate opponents.

Sample Run

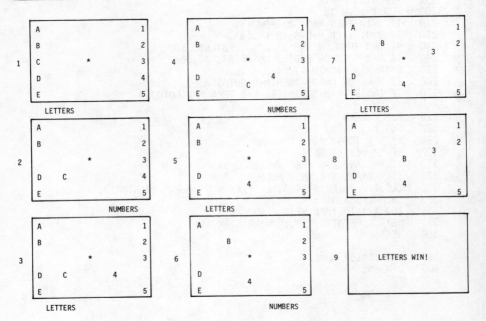

SOCCER II PROGRAM

Variables

The same as for SOCCER I with the following additions:

S(N)   strength

Program Listing

The same as for SOCCER I with the following changes:

To replace the dot indicator with the word, LETTERS, and to add the ball in the middle of the field, eliminate :SET(0,47) from line 50 and add line 52.

```
52    PRINT@960,"LETTERS";PRINT@481,"*";:PRINT@990,"I";
```

Add line 40 to draw two horizontal and two vertical lines.

```
40    FOR I=4 TO 123:SET(I,2):SET(I,42):NEXT:FOR I=2 TO 42:
      SET(4,I):SET(123,I):NEXT
```

Add lines 72 and 74 to insure that the correct characters are entered from the keyboard.

```
72    IF P=1 AND (N<65 OR N>69)THEN 60
74    IF P=2 AND (N<49 OR N>53)THEN 60
```

To make sure that an eliminated player is not moved, add line 85.

```
85    IF L(N)<0 THEN 60
```

To print characters and directional arrows on the screen, add the following lines.

```
 92    PRINT@990,X;
111    I=0
112    IF D=8 PRINT@990,CHR$(93);:I=1
114    IF D=9 PRINT@990,CHR$(94);:I=1
116    IF D=10 PRINT@990,CHR$(92);:I=1
118    IF D=91 PRINT@990,CHR$(91);:I=1
120    IF I=0 PRINT@990,"?";
```

To stop movement of player, add the following lines.

```
205    Y=INKEY$:IF Y=""THEN Y="Z"
207    IF ASC(Y)=32 THEN 400
```

Add the following to the end of line 400.

:PRINT@990,"I";

To win, add line 272.

```
272    IF M=481 GOTO 330
```

To have the movement and elimination of other players depend upon the strength, make the following additions and changes.

In line 200, replace 1Ø with S(N).

Add lines 325 and 327.

```
325    IF S(N) =S(K) THEN L(K)=-1:GOTO34Ø
327    GOTO 34Ø
```

Add line 440 to adjust strength.

```
440    FOR J=1TO1Ø:S(J)=S(J)+3:NEXT J:S(N)=S(N)-I
```

To print "LETTERS" and "NUMBERS", change lines 420 and 430 as follows.

```
420    IF P=1 THEN PRINT@96Ø,"LETTERS";:PRINT@1Ø16,"        ";
430    IF P=2 THEN PRINT@1Ø16,"NUMBERS";:PRINT@96Ø,"        ";
```

Program Listing

```
  5    REM SET
 10    (See Soccer I)
 20    FOR I=1TO1Ø:READ L(I):S(I)=5:NEXT
 30
 -
 35    (See Soccer I)
 40    FOR I=4TO123:SET(I,2):SET(I,42):NEXT:FOR I=2TO42:SET(4,I):
       SET(123,I):NEXT
 50    (See Soccer I)
 52    PRINT@96Ø,"LETTERS";:PRINT@481,"*";
 55
 -
 70    (See Soccer I)
 72    IF P=1 AND (N<65OR N>69) THEN 60
 74    IF P=2 AND (N<49 OR N>53 THEN 6Ø
 80    (See Soccer I)
 85    IF L(N)<Ø THEN 6Ø
 90    (See Soccer I)
 92    PRINT@99Ø,X;
100
 -
110    (See Soccer I)
111    I=Ø
112    IF D=8 PRINT@99Ø,CHR$(93);:I=1
114    IF D=9 PRINT@99Ø,CHR$(94);:I=1
116    IF D=1Ø PRINT@99Ø,CHR$(92);:I=1
118    IF D=91 PRINT@99Ø,CHR$(91);:I=1
120    IF I=Ø PRINT@99Ø,"?";
195    (See Soccer I)
200    FOR I=1TO S(N)
205    Y=INKEY$:IF Y="" THEN Y="Z"
207    IF ASC(Y)=32 THEN4ØØ
210
 -
270    (See Soccer I)
272    IF M=481 GOTO33Ø
```

```
275
  -
320    (See Soccer I)
325    IF S(N)>=S(K) THEN L(K)=-1:GOTO340
327    GOTO340
330.
  -
395    (See Soccer I)
400    L(N)=M:PRINT@990,"I"
410    (See Soccer I)
420    IF P=1 THEN PRINT@960,"LETTERS";:PRINT@1016,"        ";
430    IF P=2 THENPRINT@1016,"NUMBERS";:PRINT@960,"        ";
440    FOR J=1TO10:S(I)=S(J)+3:NEXT J:S(N)=S(N)-I
450
  -
506    (See Soccer I)
```

Soccer III

This program is an expansion of the previous program, SOCCER II.
SOCCER II should be working well before one begins to develop SOCCER III.

Scenario

The movement of the players in SOCCER III is the same as in the
previous program, SOCCER II. In order to win in SOCCER III, however, one
of your players must kick the ball across the opponent's goal line. The
distance the ball is kicked will depend on the strength of the player.
When eliminated, a player appears on the sideline. Strength is not a
factor in eliminating opponents as in SOCCER II, since it might be
possible for an opponent to block the movement of the ball indefinitely.

Sample Screen Display

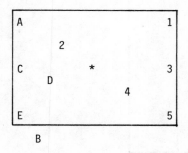 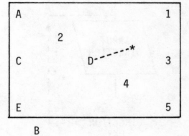

SOCCER II AND III FLOWCHART

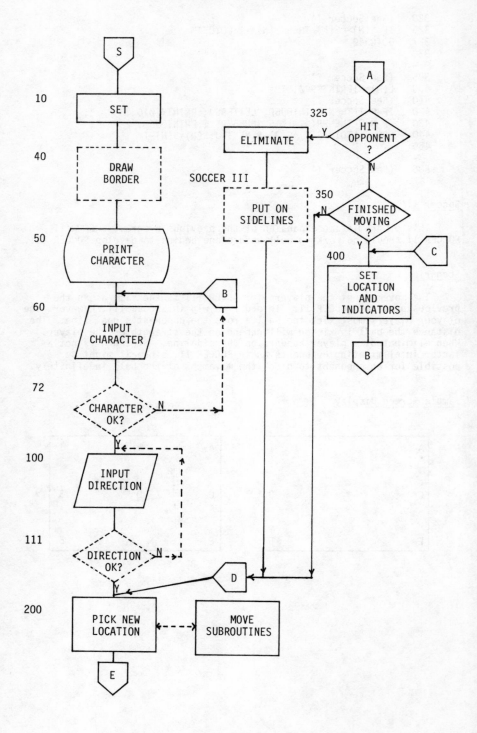

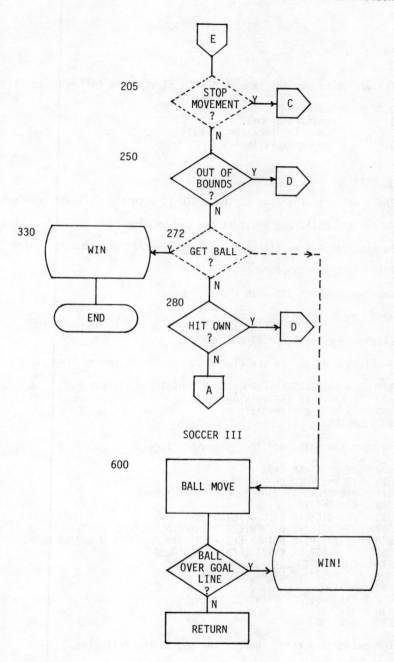

SOCCER III PROGRAM

Variables

The variables are the same as SOCCER II with the following additions.

Q,T	Indices
B	Location of ball
C	Temporary location of ball
G,H	Temporary variables

Program Listing

The listing is the same as in SOCCER II with the following changes.

To set the ball, add B=481 at the end of line 1∅.

To check if the ball is hit, replace line 272 with the following

```
272   IF M=B THEN6∅∅
```

and replace line 330 with the following.

```
330   GOSUB47∅
```

Eliminate lines 325, 327 and 335.

To place a player on the sideline, add the following lines.

```
470   Z="ABCDE12345":FOR Q=1TO K:Y=MID$(Z,Q,1):NEXT Q
480   L(K)=-9:IF K<6 PRINT@993+2*K,Y;
490   IF K>5 PRINT@993+2*K,Y;
495   RETURN
```

To move the ball, add the following lines.

```
600   IF P=1 THEN G=3
610   IF P=2 THEN G=-3
615   H=64*(RND(3)-2)
620   FOR T=1 TO S(N)/5
630   C=B+G:C=C+H:E=(C-3)/64:F=(C+4)/64
640   IF INT(E)-E=∅ THEN CLS:PRINT@41∅,"NUMBERS WIN";:GOTO64∅
650   IF INT(F)-F=∅ THEN CLS:PRINT@41∅,"LETTERS WIN";:GOTO65∅
660   IF C<127 OR C>831 THEN M=L:GOTO28∅
670   FOR Q=1 TO 1∅
680   IF C=L(Q) THEN M=L:GOTO28∅
690   NEXT Q
700   PRINT@B," ";:PRINT@C,"*";:B=C
710   NEXT T
720   GOTO28∅
```

For better blocking, change line 680 to the following.

```
680   IF C=L(Q) OR C=L(Q)+64 OR C=L(Q)-64 THEN M=L:GOTO28∅
```

SOCCER III MODIFICATIONS

Modifications with Instructions

The following modifications are not absolutely necessary but provide the reader with a variety of interesting options.

To add directions, insert the following lines.

```
2    CLS:PRINT@389,"WANT INSTRUCTIONS (Y OR N)";
4    Y$=INKEY$:IF Y$=""THEN 4
6    IF Y$="Y"THEN GOSUB800

800  PRINT"TO WIN GET * ACROSS GOAL."
801  PRINT"* MOVES TOWARD GOAL WHEN TOUCHED BY PLAYER."
802  PRINT"TO MOVE PLAYER, PRESS LETTER OR NUMERAL THEN ARROW."
803  PRINT"STOP PLAYER BY PRESSING SPACE BAR."
804  PRINT"PLAYER IS OUT OF GAME IF HIT BY OPPONENT."
805  PRINT"PLAYERS BLOCK *."
806  PRINT"DISTANCE PLAYER MOVES AND BALL GOES DEPENDS ON STRENGTH."
807  PRINT"PLAYER LOSES STRENGTH WHEN MOVING.  GAINS STRENGTH WHEN
     RESTING."
808  PRINT"TEAM THAT KICKS BALL MAINTAINS CONTROL."
809  PRINT"PRESS ANY KEY TO PLAY."
810  Y$=INKEY$:IF Y$=""THEN810
811  RETURN
```

To allow the player who kicks the ball another chance to dribble or pass, add the following line.

```
720  L(N)=M:PRINT@L," ";:PRINT@M,X;:GOTO60
```

To make the ball easier to hit, add the following line.

```
272  IF M=B OR M=B-3 OR M=B+3 OR M=B-61 OR M=B-67 OR M=B+67 OR
     M=B+64 OR M=B-64 THEN 600
```

To keep score, add the following lines.

```
640  IF INT(E)-I=0 THEN PRINT@410,"NUMBERS SCORE";:NS=NS+1:GOTO750
650  IF INT(F)-F=0 THEN PRINT@410,"LETTERS SCORE";:LS=LS+1:GOTO750
750  FOR I=1 TO 1000:NEXT
760  PRINT:PRINT"LETTERS:";LS:PRINT"NUMBERS:";NS:FOR I=1 TO 2000:
     NEXT:GOTO 10
```

To keep time, add the following lines.

```
450  TT=TT+1:PRINT@995,TT;
452  IF TT>100THEN CLS:IF LS>NS PRINT@410,"LETTERS WIN":END ELSE
     PRINT@410,"NUMBERS WIN":END
```

Modifications

1. Injured players on the sideline return after three or four moves.
2. Provide a goal keeper.
3. Use a timer and scoring device.
4. Add more players.
5. Implement regulation soccer rules.
6. Allow passing to teammates.

ART AUCTION

Scenario

In this simulation, you will be given an opportunity to buy and sell up to five paintings. The objective is to make a large profit by buying the paintings for as little as possible and selling them for as much as possible.

In order to buy a painting, you must bid against a secret bid made by another buyer (the computer). When a painting is offered for sale, three numbers will be given that represent the mean and range of bids for this particular painting. For example, "200 300 400" indicates that the mean bid price for the painting is 300, and about 70% of the time the price will be between 200 and 400. (Note that higher priced paintings tend to have a larger range of prices.)

After you buy your paintings, you will be given an opportunity to sell them. You will receive from one to five offers, but you do not know in advance how many offers will be made. The offers will be, on the average, 50 higher than the bids made during the buying phase. If you do not accept an offer, and it is the last one, then the offer will be automatically processed. Sometimes it will be wise to accept an offer that is less than the purchase price rather than gamble on a higher offer that does not materialize.

When all of the paintings that you have bought have been sold, you will be given your total profit for all of the transactions.

Sample Run

```
BUY PAINTING  1
PRICES:  546  553  560
YOUR BID?  560
OPPONENT BID  565.
YOU WERE OUT BID.

BUY PAINTING  2
PRICES:  336  449  562
YOUR BID?  400
OPPONENT BID  440.
YOU WERE OUT BID.

BUY PAINTING  3
PRICES:  213  288  363
YOUR BID?  300
OPPONENT BID  324
YOU WERE OUT BID.

BUY PAINTING  4
PRICES:  403  514  625
YOUR BID?  600
OPPONENT BID  497.
YOU BOUGHT IT.
```

```
BUY PAINTING  5
PRICES:  274  346  417
YOUR BID?  350
OPPONENT BID  311.
YOU BOUGHT IT.

SELL PAINTING  4
YOU BOUGHT IT FOR  600.
AVERAGE OFFER IS  564.
OFFER 1 IS  649.
ACCEPT?  Y

SELL PAINTING  5
YOU BOUGHT IT FOR  350.
AVERAGE OFFER IS  396.
OFFER 1 IS 365.
ACCEPT?  N

YOUR PROFIT IS  64.
PLAY AGAIN?
```

ART AUCTION PROGRAM

Variables

P(5)	Prices
S(5)	Price range
F(5)	Set flag if painting is bought
CB	Opponent's bid
YB	Your bid
I,J,K	Indices
P	Profit
N	Number
D	Dividend
Q	Quotient

Program Listing

```
5        REM SET PRICES AND RANGES
10       DIM P(5),S(5),F(5)
20       FOR I=1 TO 5
30       P(I)=100+INT(900*RND(1))
40       S(I)=INT(P(I)*RND(1))
50       IF P(I)<500 THEN S(I)=INT(P(I)*.7*RND(1))
60       F(I)=0
70       NEXT I

95       REM BUY PAINTINGS
100      FOR I=1 TO 5
110      GO SUB 500
120      PRINT: PRINT "BUY PAINTING"; I:PRINT:PRINT
130      PRINT "PRICES:"; INT(P(I)-.5*S(I)); P(I); INT(P(I)+.5*S(I))
140      PRINT: PRINT: INPUT "YOUR BID"; YB
150      PRINT "OPPONENT"S BID"; CB; "."
160      IF YB>CB THEN PRINT "YOU BOUGHT IT.": F(I)=YB: GO TO 180
170      PRINT "YOU WERE OUT BID."
180      NEXT I

195      REM SELL PAINTINGS
200      FOR I=1 TO 5
210      IF F(I)=0 THEN 310
220      FOR K=1 TO INT(5*RND(1))
230      GO SUB 500: CB=CB+INT(100*RND(1))

240      PRINT "SELL PAINTINGS"; I
250      PRINT "YOU BOUGHT IT FOR"; F(I): PRINT "AVERAGE OFFER IS";
         P(I)+50
260      PRINT "OFFER"; K; "IS"; CB; "."
270      INPUT "ACCEPT"; Y$
280      IF Y$="Y" THEN 300
290      NEXT K
300      P=P+CB-F(I)
310      NEXT I
320      PRINT: PRINT "YOUR PROFIT IS"; P; "."
330      INPUT "PLAY AGAIN"; Y$
340      IF Y$="Y" THEN RUN
350      END
```

```
495   REM NORMAL DISTRIBUTION SUBROUTINE
500   D=0
510   N=INT(65536*RND(1))
520   FOR J=1 TO 16
530   Q=INT(N/2)
540   D=D+2*(N/2-Q)
550   N=Q
560   NEXT J
570   CB=P(I)+S(I)*(D-8)/8
580   CB=CB+20*RND(1)
590   CB=INT(CB)
600   RETURN
```

ART AUCTION MODIFICATIONS

Minor

1. Number of paintings -- lines 10, 20, 100, 200
2. Starting prices -- line 30
3. Price spread -- lines 40, 50
4. Built-in profit -- lines 230, 250
5. Error in price range -- line 580
6. Number of offers -- line 220

Major

1. Have one or more of the paintings a forgery that is worth nothing.
2. Have one or more of the paintings that have a low purchase price be very valuable.
3. Have more opponents bid against you.

ART AUCTION FLOWCHART

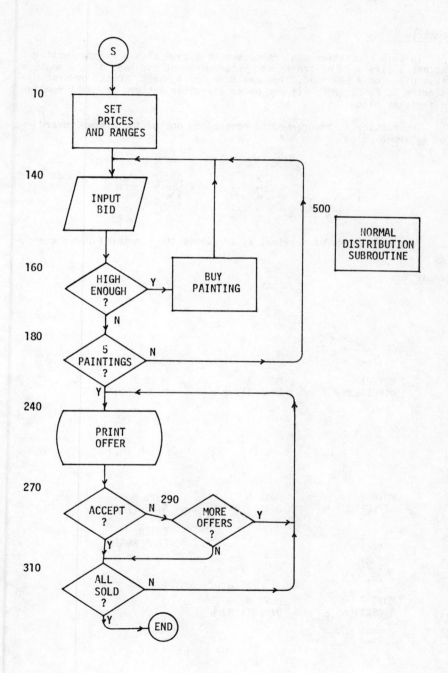

MONSTER CHASE

Scenario

In this simulation you are locked in a cage with a hungry monster who has a life span of ten turns. Your movement and that of the monster takes place on a 5X5 grid. You may move north, east, south, or west by entering N, E, S, or W. If you enter any other letter, you will remain in the same place.

The monster is programmed to move along one of the arrows toward you as shown below :

Your only means of survival is to outwit the monster for ten turns.

Sample Run

```
M . . . .
. . . . .
. . . . .
. . . . .
. . . . Y
```

MOVE 1
DIRECTION? W

```
. M . . .
. . . . .
. . . . .
. . . Y .
```

MOVE 2
DIRECTION? N

```
. . . . .
. . M . .
. . . Y .
. . . . .
```

MOVE 3
DIRECTION? S

```
. . . . .
. . . M .
. . . Y .
```

MOVE 4
DIRECTION? W

```
. . . . .
. . . . .
. . . M .
. . Y . .
```

MOVE 5
DIRECTION? W

```
. . . . .
. . . . .
. Y . M .
```

MOVE 6
DIRECTION? N

```
. . . . . .
. . . . . .
. Y M . . .
. . . . . .
```

MOVE 7
DIRECTION? W

```
. . . . .
Y M . . .
. . . . .
```

MOVE 8
DIRECTION? N

EATEN
PLAY AGAIN?

MONSTER CHASE PROGRAM

Variables

R,C	Your row and column
X,Y	Monster's row and column
L,M	Temporary variables
M$	Your move (N,E,S,W,O)
D	Direction of the monster (1-8)
T	Turns (1-10)

Listing

```
5       REM SET CONDITIONS
10      X=1: Y=1
20      R=5: C=5
30      FOR T=1 TO 10

35      REM DISPLAY GRID
40      FOR I=1 TO 5
50      FOR J=1 TO 5
60      PRINT TAB(8)
70      IF I=X AND J=Y THEN PRINT "M";: GO TO 100
80      IF I=R AND J=C THEN PRINT "Y";: GO TO 100
90      PRINT ".";
100     NEXT J
110     PRINT
120     NEXT I

210     ?:?:? "MOVE NUMBER"; T
220     INPUT "DIRECTION (NESWO)"; M$
240     IF M$="N" THEN R=R-1
250     IF M$="E" THEN C=C+1
260     IF M$="S" THEN R=R+1
270     IF M$="W" THEN C=C-1
280     IF R*C=0 OR R>5 OR C>5 THEN PRINT "OUT OF BOUNDS": GO TO 520
290     IF R=X AND Y=C THEN PRINT "EATEN": GO TO 520
300     IF X=R AND Y<C THEN D=1
310     IF X>R AND Y<C THEN D=2
320     IF X>R AND Y=C THEN D=3
330     IF X>R AND Y>C THEN D=4
340     IF X=R AND Y>C THEN D=5
350     IF X<R AND Y>C THEN D=6
360     IF X<R AND Y=C THEN D=7
370     IF X<R AND Y<C THEN D=8
380     D=D+INT(3*RND(1)-1)
390     IF D=0 THEN D=8
400     IF D=9 THEN D=1
410     IF D>1 AND D<5 THEN X=X-1
420     IF D>5 THEN X=X+1
430     IF D>3 AND D<7 THEN Y=Y-1
440     IF D<3 OR D=8 THEN Y=Y+1
450     IF X=0 THEN X=X+1
460     IF Y=0 THEN Y=Y+1
470     IF X=6 THEN X=X-1
480     IF Y=6 THEN Y=Y-1
```

```
490    IF X=R AND Y=C THEN PRINT "EATEN": GO TO 520
500    NEXT T
510    PRINT "YOU SURVIVED!"
520    INPUT "PLAY AGAIN"; Y$
530    IF Y$="Y" THEN RUN
540    END
```

MONSTER CHASE MODIFICATIONS

Minor

1. Grid size -- lines 20, 40, 50, 280, 470, 480
2. Turns to win -- line 30

Major

1. Have more than one monster.
2. Chase a little monster while a big monster tries to get you.
3. Have the monster fall in quicksand.
4. Require food in order to maintain energy.

MONSTER CHASE FLOWCHART

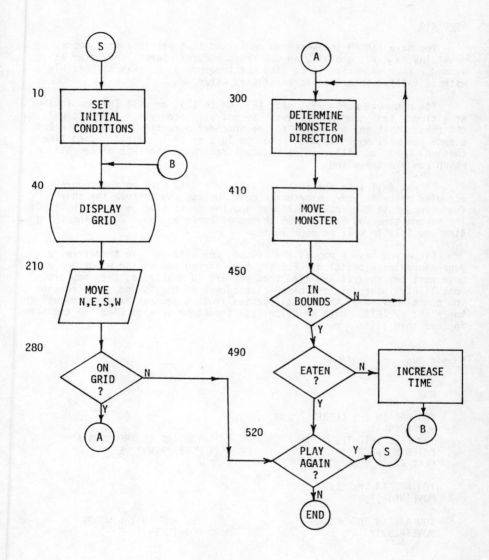

LOST TREASURE

Scenario

You have landed somewhere on an island that has treasure, woods, mountains, a cave, a bluff, an oak tree, and, of course, sea water all around. Your objective is to find the treasure as quickly as possible without falling into the shark-infested water.

You can move north (N), east (E), south (S), or west (W) one square at a time. Your compass, however, is not very accurate. There is only an 80% chance that you will move in the intended direction. There is a 20% chance you will move diagonally to the left or to the right. Each time that you move you will receive feedback regarding the type of terrain on which you are traveling.

If you fall into the sea, you will be placed back on the square occupied prior to your unfortunate move, unless you disturb the sharks. The chance that the sharks will eat you the first time you fall in is 20%. The second time you fall in the chance of being eaten is 70%. The third time you fall in will be your last!

Since you have a map of the island, you will be able to determine your approximate position. For example, if you are in the woods and you move east two squares and find that you are in mountains, then you are most likely located in the north-east corner of the island. The reason you can't be sure of the exact location is that you may have veered off to the right or left. With practice, you should be able to find the treasure in less than fifteen moves.

Sample Run

```
RUN

YOU ARE IN THE CLEAR.                    .
MOVE(NESW)?  S                           .
YOU FELL INTO THE OCEAN.        YOU ARE IN THE MOUNTAINS.
EATEN BY SHARK.                 MOVE(NESW)?  E
PLAY AGAIN Y OR N?  Y

YOU ARE IN THE CLEAR.                    .
MOVE(NESW)?  S                           .
                                         .
YOU ARE IN THE WOODS.           YOU ARE IN THE WOODS.
MOVE(NESW)?  N                  MOVE(NESW)?  S

    .                                    .
    .                                    .
    .                                    .

                                YOU ARE IN THE CLEAR.
                                MOVE(NESW)?  E
                                YOU FOUND THE TREASURE IN 9 MOVES.
                                PLAY AGAIN Y OR N?
```

LOST TREASURE FLOWCHART

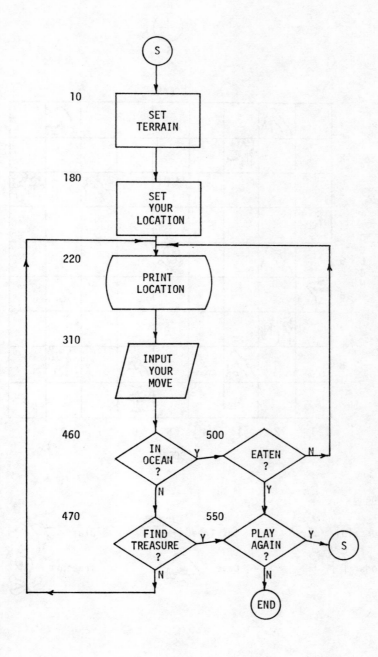

LOST TREASURE MAP

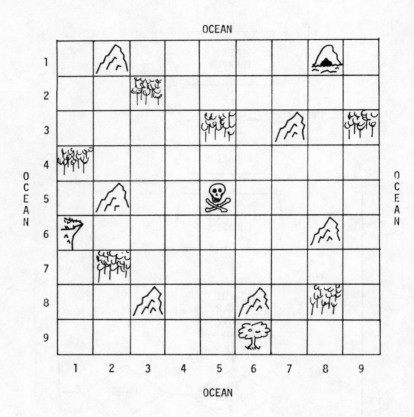

Legend

Mountains   Oak Tree   Bluff

Woods   Cave   Treasure

LOST TREASURE PROGRAM

Variables

L(R,C)	Locations
S	Probability of being eaten by shark
R	Your row
C	Your column
RT, CT	Temporary storage
T	Number of turns

Listing

```
5     REM SET TERRAIN
10    DIM L(9,9)
20    S=.2
30    FOR I=1 TO 9: FOR J=1 TO 9
40    L(I,J)=0
50    NEXT J,I

60    FOR I=1 TO 6
70    READ R,C
80    L(R,C)=1
90    NEXT I

100   FOR I=1 TO 6
110   READ R,C
120   L(R,C)=2
130   NEXT I

140   L(1,8)=3
150   L(6,1)=4
160   L(9,6)=5
170   L(5,5)=6

175   REM YOUR LOCATION
180   R=INT(9*RND(1)+1)
190   C=INT(9*RND(1)+1)
200   IF SQR((R-5)↑2+(C-5)↑2)<2 THEN 180

205   REM START MAIN LOOP
210   FOR T=1 TO 100
220   PRINT "YOU ARE ";
230   J=L(R,C)+1
240   ON J GO SUB 250,260,270,280,290,300:  GO TO 310
250   PRINT "IN THE CLEAR.": RETURN
260   PRINT "IN THE WOODS.": RETURN
270   PRINT "IN THE MOUNTAINS.": RETURN
280   PRINT "NEAR A CAVE.": RETURN
290   PRINT "ON A BLUFF.": RETURN
300   PRINT "NEAR AN OAK TREE.": RETURN

310   INPUT "MOVE(NESW)"; M$
320   RT=R: CT=C
330   IF M$="N" THEN R=R-1: GO SUB 380
340   IF M$="E" THEN C=C+1: GO SUB 420
350   IF M$="W" THEN C=C-1: GO SUB 420
360   IF M$="S" THEN R=R+1: GO SUB 380
```

```
370   GO TO 460

375   REM MOVE SUBROUTINE
380   J=INT(10*RND(1)+1)
390   IF J>2 THEN RETURN
400   IF J=1 THEN C=C+1: RETURN
410   C=C-1: RETURN
420   J=INT(10*RND(1)+1)
430   IF J>2 THEN RETURN
440   IF J=1 THEN R=R+1: RETURN
450   R=R-1: RETURN

455   REM IN OCEAN, FOUND TREASURE?
460   IF R<1 OR R>9 OR C<1 OR C>9 THEN 490
470   IF L(R,C)=6 THEN PRINT "YOU FOUND THE TREASURE IN"; T: GO TO 550
480   NEXT T

490   PRINT "YOU FELL INTO THE OCEAN."
500   IF RND(1)<S THEN PRINT "EATEN BY SHARKS!": GO TO 550
510   S=S+.5: R=RT: C=CT: IF S>1 THEN S=1
520   PRINT "THE PROBABILITY OF BEING EATEN"
530   PRINT "BY A SHARK NEXT TIME IS"; S; "."
540   GO TO 480

550   INPUT "PLAY AGAIN"; Y$
560   IF Y$="Y" THEN RUN
570   END

580   DATA 2,3,3,5,3,9,4,1,7,2,8,8
590   DATA 1,2,3,7,5,2,6,8,8,3,8,6
```

LOST TREASURE MODIFICATIONS

Minor

1. Probability of first shark attack -- line 20
2. Grid size -- lines 30, 180, 190, 460
3. Number of woods -- lines 60, 580
4. Number of mountains -- lines 100, 590
5. Landmarks' locations -- lines 140, 150, 160
6. Location of the treasure -- line 170
7. Movement error -- lines 380, 420
8. Amount you disturb shark -- line 510

Major

1. Vary number and amount of treasure.
2. Add parameters of water and/or food to maintain your energy level.
3. Hunt a moving treasure.
4. Modify direction of movement.
5. Add quicksand.
6. Include landmarks placed at random that are not on the map.
7. Randomly place treasure before each hunt.

NOTES

GONE FISHING

You are going on a fishing trip. The sea is an 8X8 grid, forming 64 fishing locations. You will start at the dock, square (1,1), and try to catch as many pounds of fish as you can. You may move one square at a time horizontally or vertically by entering a north(N), south(S), east(E), or west(W). Entering an F allows you to fish in the same place again, and a B allows you to start another fishing trip immediately. If you select a direction that takes you off the grid, your ship will sink. You must return to the dock in sixty moves, which is equivalent to six hours. If you don't return in time, half of your catch will spoil.

The chance of catching fish is different for each square and is determined at the beginning of the trip. The chance of catching fish in a given square will remain the same throughout the trip or will decrease if the fish are scared by a shark. The maximum number of fish that can be caught in each square (density) is also determined at the beginning of the simulation. This number varies from 1 to 5. The maximum number of fish you can catch in a square will decrease only if sea gulls eat some of the bait. The maximum weight of a fish in a particular square is the product of the row and column; therefore, the further out you go, the bigger the fish.

The longer you fish, the greater the chance of an afternoon storm occurring. If you hit a storm, you will lose .5 hour. One of the more difficult manuvers of the trip is to fish as long as necessary to accumulate a large catch without getting lost in a storm. Also, there is a 4% chance that you will experience some unexpected event during each move of the trip. Be sure you return to the dock before six hours have elapsed. Your rating as a fisherman will be the number of pounds of fish you catch divided by five.

You may wish to use the fishing grid on page 4.6 to record the best fishing spots. A small marker can be used to keep track of your location on the grid.

Sample Run

```
RUN

NO BITES
AT LOCATION  1  1
TOTAL LBS. THIS TRIP IS 0.
YOU HAVE FISHED FOR 0 HOURS.
MOVE(N,S,E,W,F,B)?  E

NO BITES
AT LOCATION  1  2
TOTAL LBS. THIS TRIP IS 0.
YOU HAVE FISHED FOR .1 HOURS.
MOVE(N,S,E,W,F,B)?  S

YOU CAUGHT 1 FISH,
EACH WEIGHING 2 LBS.
AT LOCATION  2  2
TOTAL LBS. THIS TRIP IS 2.
YOU HAVE FISHED FOR .2 HOURS.
MOVE(N,S,E,W,F,B)?  S

NO BITES
AT LOCATION  3  2
TOTAL LBS. THIS TRIP IS 2.
YOU HAVE FISHED FOR .3 HOURS.
MOVE(N,S,E,W,F,B)?  E

YOU CAUGHT 4 FISH,
EACH WEIGHING 2 LBS.
AT LOCATION  3  3
TOTAL LBS. THIS TRIP IS 10.
YOU HAVE FISHED FOR .4 HOURS.
MOVE(N,S,E,W,F,B)?  E

    .
    .
NO BITES
AT LOCATION  4  6
TOTAL LBS. THIS TRIP IS 10.
SEA GULLS ATE SOME OF YOUR BAIT.
CATCH WILL BE SMALLER THIS TRIP.
YOU HAVE FISHED FOR .8 HOURS.
MOVE(N,S,E,W,F,B)?  S

    .
    .
```

```
    .
    .
    .
YOU CAUGHT 4 FISH,
EACH WEIGHING 15 LBS.
AT LOCATION  4  8
TOTAL LBS. THIS TRIP IS 155.
YOU CAUGHT A 50 LB. SHARK.
TOTAL LBS. THIS TRIP IS 205.
YOU HAVE FISHED FOR 1.8 HOURS.
MOVE(N,S,E,W,F,B)?  W

    .
    .
    .
YOU CAUGHT 1 FISH,
EACH WEIGHING 3 LBS.
AT LOCATION  3  3
TOTAL LBS. THIS TRIP IS 208.
WATER SPOUT DISPLACES YOU.
YOU ARE NOW AT LOCATION  4  5
YOU HAVE FISHED FOR 2.6 HOURS.
MOVE(N,S,E,W,F,B)?  W

    .
    .
    .
NO BITES
AT LOCATION  1  2
TOTAL LBS. THIS TRIP IS 211.
YOU HAVE FISHED FOR 3.2 HOURS.
MOVE(N,S,E,W,F,B)?  W

YOU ARE BACK AT THE DOCK
AFTER 3.2 HOURS OF FISHING
CLEAN 211 LBS. OF FISH.
YOU RATE 42 AS A FISHERMAN.
```

GONE FISHING FLOWCHART

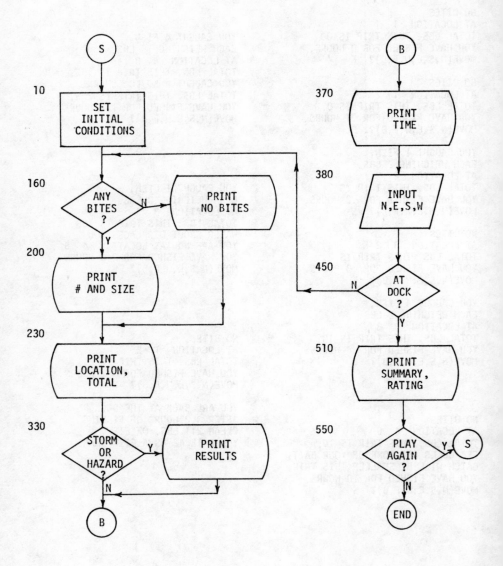

GONE FISHING PROGRAM

Variables

P(I,J)	The probability of catching a fish
D(I,J)	The maximum number of fish in square (I,J), from 1 to 5
W	Weight of each fish caught, from 1 to RXC
P	The total number of pounds of fish caught at a given time
R	Row in which you are fishing
C	Column in which you are fishing
N	Number of fish caught in a given turn
T	Time in tenths of an hour, maximum 6 hours
M$	Move(N,E,S,W,F,B), where N,E,S, and W are directions, F allows you to fish again in the same square, and B allows you to start the fishing trip over again

Listing

```
5       REM SET PROBABILITIES AND DENSITY
10      DIM P(8,8),D(8,8)
20      FOR I=1 TO 8: FOR J=1 TO 8
30      P(I,J)=.7*RND(1)
40      D(I,J)=INT(RND(1)*5+1)
50      NEXT J,I
60      P(1,1)=0: P=0: R=1: C=1

145     REM MAIN LOOP
150     FOR T=0 TO 6 STEP .1
160     IF RND(1)>P(R,C) OR D(R,C)<1 THEN PRINT "NO BITES": GO TO 220
170     N=INT(RND(1)*D(R,C)+1)
180     W=INT(RND(1)*R*C)+1
190     P=P+N*W
200     PRINT "YOU CAUGHT"; N; "FISH,"
210     PRINT "EACH WEIGHING"; W; "LBS.,"
220     PRINT "AT LOCATION"; R; C
230     PRINT "TOTAL LBS. THIS TRIP IS"; P; "."

325     REM UNEXPECTED EXPERIENCES
330     IF RND(1)<T/60 THEN PRINT "STORM -- LOST 1/2 HOUR": T=T+.5
340     J=INT(100*RND(1))+1
350     IF J>4 THEN 370
360     ON J GO SUB 600,700,800,900

370     PRINT "YOU HAVE FISHED FOR"; T; "HOURS."
380     INPUT "MOVE (N,S,E,W,F,B)"; M$
390     IF M$="E" THEN C=C+1
400     IF M$="N" THEN R=R-1
410     IF M$="W" THEN C=C-1
420     IF M$="S" THEN R=R+1
430     IF M$="B" THEN RUN
440     IF R<1 OR R>8 OR C<1 OR C>8 THEN PRINT "GROUNDED--SUNK!":  GO TO 550
450     IF R=1 AND C=1 THEN GO TO 500
460     NEXT T

470     PRINT "TIME UP. THE SUN HAS SET."
480     PRINT "HALF OF YOUR CATCH HAS SPOILED."
490     P=P/2
```

```
495    REM SUMMARY OF TRIP
500    IF T=0 THEN PRINT "STILL AT DOCK": GO TO 10
510    PRINT "YOU ARE BACK AT THE DOCK"
520    PRINT "AFTER"; T; "HOURS OF FISHING."
530    PRINT "CLEAN"; P; "LBS. OF FISH."
540    "YOU RATE"; INT(P/5); "AS A FISHERMAN."
550    INPUT "ANOTHER FISHING TRIP(Y,N)"; X$
560    IF X$="Y" THEN RUN
570    END

595    REM SUBROUTINES
600    IF R+C<9 THEN RETURN
610    PRINT "FISH SCARED BY SHARK."
620    PRINT "NOT BITING AS OFTEN."
630    FOR I=1 TO 8: FOR J=1 TO 8
640    P(I,J)=P(I,J)-.1
650    NEXT J,I
660    RETURN
700    PRINT "SEA GULLS ATE SOME OF YOUR BAIT."
710    PRINT "CATCH WILL BE SMALLER THIS TRIP."
720    FOR I=1 TO 8; FOR J=1 TO 8
730    D(I,J)=D(I,J)-1
740    NEXT J,I
750    RETURN
800    PRINT "WATER SPOUT DISPLACES YOU."
810    R=INT(8*RND(1)+1)
820    C=INT(8*RND(1)+1)
830    PRINT "YOU ARE NOW AT LOCATION"; R; C
840    T=T+.2
850    RETURN
900    PRINT "YOU CAUGHT A 50 LB. SHARK."
910    P=P+50
920    PRINT "TOTAL LBS. THIS TRIP IS"; P; "."
930    RETURN
```

GONE FISHING MODIFICATIONS

Minor

1. Grid size -- lines 10, 20, 440, 630, 720, 810, and 820
2. Maximum probability of catching fish in a square -- line 30
3. Maximum density of fish in a square -- line 40
4. Maximum time of fishing -- line 150
5. Storm probability -- line 330
6. Rating scale -- line 540

Major

1. Catch different kinds of fish, such as, sharks, whales, or mermaids.
2. Change the goal to catching the biggest fish.
3. Use fuel to run the boat.
4. Add a choice of hook sizes and fishing depth.
5. Add different kinds of hazards, such as whales, reefs, UFO's.
6. Let fishing success depend on time of day.
7. Fix weather conditions and fishing conditions at the beginning of the trip.
8. Utilize sonar devices to help locate fish.
9. Allow ship to move in a diagonal direction.

FISHING MAP

	1	2	3	4	5	6	7	8
1								
2								
3								
4								
5								
6								
7								
8								

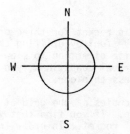

SPACE FLIGHT

Scenario

In this simulation, you are living in the year 2062 as the captain of a space ship. Your orders are to deliver medical supplies from Alpha at coordinates (10,10) to Beta at coordinates (80,80). Your rating as a space pilot will depend upon how fast you can make the trip.

During each time interval, you will be able to determine the following information:

1. Total time elapsed
2. Location in terms of X and Y coordinates
3. Amount of fuel left
4. Speed
5. The angle at which you are moving
6. Your distance from the planet.

To change direction or to increase or decrease speed, you can fire one of two kinds of rockets: main (M) and half (H). These rockets take one unit and 1/2 unit of fuel, respectively. A "C" will allow you to coast for five time intervals.

Once you decide how much fuel you are going to burn, you must decide on the direction in which you will be firing the rockets. You are able to rotate your space ship with small thrusters as it drifts in space. The directions are shown below:

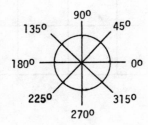

Once you fire your main rocket for three or four turns to increase your speed, you can conserve fuel by drifting through space. You must start to fire in the opposite direction to slow down before arriving at Beta. In order to meet arrival conditions, you must be within a distance of one and at a speed of less than one.

You may wish to make copies of the grid at the end of this section to aid in plotting your course. If you find that you are off course, you may have to fire a "correction" rocket. In order to estimate the angle of firing, you can use a force diagram as shown below.

Example 1: Correction

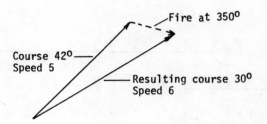

Fire at 350°

Course 42°
Speed 5

Resulting course 30°
Speed 6

Example 2: Retrofire

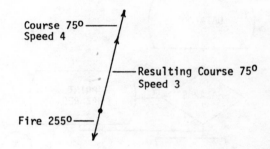

Course 75°
Speed 4

Resulting Course 75°
Speed 3

Fire 255°

Sample Run

```
              DATA READOUT
0 HOURS       10 LITERS
LOCATION   10   10
VELOCITY:  0
DEGREES:   0
D=98.995
COMMAND(O,M,H,C)?  M
ANGLE?  45


              DATA READOUT
.01 HOURS     9 LITERS
LOCATION   10.6776   10.67
VELOCITY:  .952905
DEGREES:   45
D=98.942

                .
                .
                .
```

```
                  DATA READOUT
.05 HOURS     5 LITERS
LOCATION   20.1487   20.8211
VELOCITY:  5.0035
DEGREES:   50
D=84.1685
PROBLEM SUPPORT SYSTEM
COMMAND(O,M,H,C)?  O


                .

                .

                  DATA READOUT
.33 HOURS     1 LITERS
LOCATION  79.1844   81.0019
VELOCITY:  .023181
DEGREES:   58
D=1.29189
COMMAND(O,M,H,C)?  H
ANGLE?  315
ARRIVED!
THE TRIP TOOK .33 HOURS.
YOUR RATING IS 66.
PLAY AGAIN?  N
OK
```

SPACE FLIGHT FLOWCHART

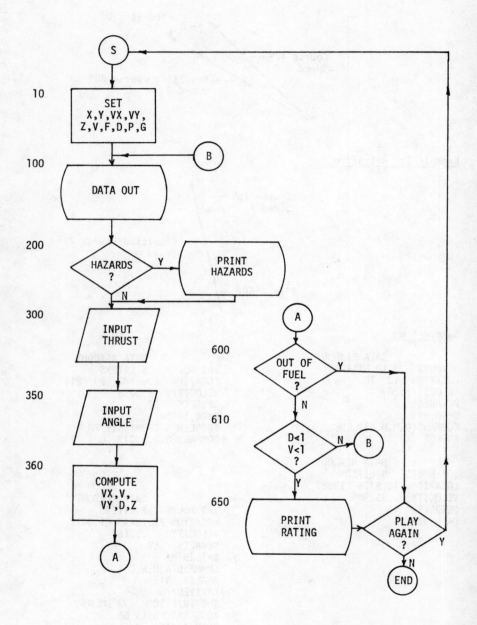

SPACE FLIGHT PROGRAM

Variables

X,Y	Location
VX,VY	Speed
Z	Angle of coast
V	Velocity
T	Time
D	Distance to planet
J	Index for hazards
F	Fuel
A	Angle input
L,M	Temporary Variables
R	Rating
F1	Coast count
G	Accuracy of gyros

Listing

```
10      X=10: Y=10: VX=0: VY=0: Z=0: V=0
20      F=10: D=98.995: P=3.1416: G=1
30      FOR T=0 TO 10 STEP .01

100     PRINT "      DATA READOUT:": ?
110     PRINT T; "HOURS          "; F; "LITERS"
120     PRINT "LOCATION:"; X; Y: PRINT "VELOCITY:"; V
130     PRINT Z; "DEGREES"
140     PRINT "DISTANCE:"; D

200     J=INT(50*RND(1)+1)
210     IF J<6 THEN PRINT "PROBLEMS: ";
220     ON J GO SUB 230,240,250,260,270: GO TO 290
230     PRINT "GYROS  ANGLE ERROR": G=G+1: RETURN
240     PRINT "FUEL LINE": F=F-.5: RETURN
250     PRINT "LIFE SUPPORT": T=T+.05: RETURN
260     PRINT "ALIENS": VX=0: VY=0: RETURN
270     PRINT "METEORS.": VX=VX+RND(1)-.5: VY=VY+RND(1)-.5
280     RETURN

290     IF F1>0 THEN F1=F1-1: GO TO 450
300     INPUT "COMMAND(O,M,H,C)"; C$
310     IF C$="M" THEN B=1: GO TO 350
320     IF C$="H" THEN B=2: GO TO 350
330     IF C$="C" THEN F1=5
340     GO TO 450
350     INPUT "ANGLE"; A: A=A+(20*G*RND(1)-10*G)
360     A=A*P/180
370     L=COS(A): M=SIN(A): F=F-1/B
380     VX=VX+(1+.4*RND(1)-.2)*L/B
390     VY=VY+(1+.4*RND(1)-.2)*M/B
400     IF VX=0 AND VY>=0 THEN Z=90: GO TO 450
410     IF VX=0 AND VY<0 THEN Z=270: GO TO 450
420     Z=ATN(VY/VX): Z=Z*180/P
430     Z=Z+INT(10*RND(1)): Z=INT(Z)
440     IF VX<0 THEN Z=Z+180
450     X=X+VX: Y=Y+VY
```

```
530    V=SQR(VX↑2+VY↑2)
540    D=SQR((X-80)↑2+(Y-80)↑2)

600    IF F<0 THEN PRINT "OUT OF FUEL": GO TO 660
610    IF D<1 AND V<1 THEN PRINT "ARRIVED": GO TO 630
620    NEXT T
630    PRINT "THE TRIP TOOK"; T; "HOURS."
640    R=200*T
650    PRINT "YOUR RATING IS"; R; "."
660    INPUT "PLAY AGAIN"; Y$
670    IF Y$="Y" THEN RUN
680    END
```

SPACE FLIGHT MODIFICATIONS

Minor

1. Starting position -- lines 10,20
2. Amount of fuel -- line 20
3. Time limit -- line 30
4. Planets location -- lines 540, 20
5. Arrival conditions -- line 610
6. Probability of problems -- line 200

Major

1. One must fire small thruster rockets to rotate ship.
2. Have meteors hit ship.
3. Use meteor shields.
4. Fight aliens.
5. Visit more than one planet.
6. Provide planets with gravitational force.
7. Have refueling stations.

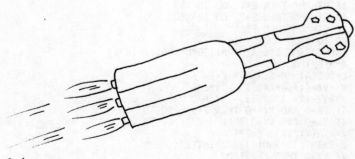

Sandy

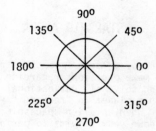

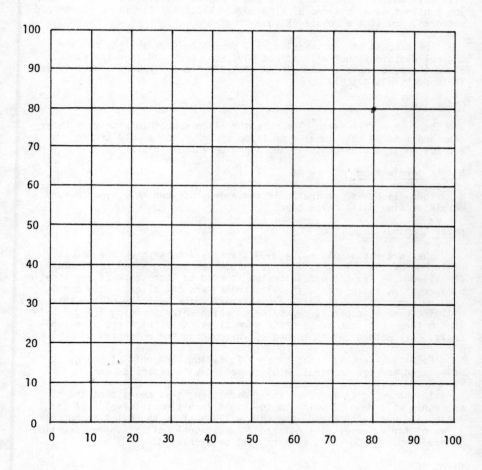

STARSHIP ALPHA

You are the commander of a large spaceship traveling to the distant planet, Omega. You must make decisions regarding the use of shields, gyros, and lazer beams and solve all navigational problems. You must choose between landing on a planet to "recharge" your engines or continuing your journey. When an alien spaceship is near, you will have to decide when to bring down your shields to perform a radar search. You will have to avoid the black hole and a planet emitting radiation. Should you continue at warp speed or slow down? Watch out for space storms and meteors! How is the morale of your crew?

The success of your mission will depend on your ability to make logical decisions that will affect you, your crew and your spaceship. Since the program is written in a "real time" mode, you will have to make these decisions quickly.

Objective

Your objective is to eliminate the alien spaceship with your lazer beam and land on the planet symbolized by "#". You should try to accomplish this mission in as short a time as possible.

Flight Termination

Your flight is terminated if the energy of your ship, your crew's morale or time falls below zero.

Motor Commands

The curser controls, ←, →, ↑, ↓, are used to turn on the motors. While one of the motors is firing, its corresponding arrow is displayed on the video. An x·y coordinate system is used to keep track of the location of your ship, the planets, the black hole, and the alien. Only one command can be given in each time-interval. The velocity of the spaceship will increase or decrease depending on which motor is being fired. Note that motors that face in opposite directions cannot be fired simultaneously. All motors can be turned off by pushing the entry key.

Each time-interval that a motor is firing, one unit of energy is being used and the temperature of the engines increases by one.

If the velocity is .2 in the x direction, this means that the spaceship will move .2 units to the right each time-interval. If the motors are not being fired, the ship will coast in space. A speed over 2 "warp" for vx or vy will utilize an additional unit of energy per time-interval and a "TOO FAST" message will be displayed.

Gyros "G"

Pressing a G key will turn on the gyros, which cost one unit of energy each turn (time-interval). The gyros will give you better control of the motor firings and the velocity will change only by .1 each time-interval, instead of the random velocity change that occurs without the gyros. The gyros will allow you to gain better control when attempting a soft landing on a planet.

Shield "S"

Pressing the S key will place an electronic shield around your spaceship. Such a shield costs one unit of energy each turn. The shield will protect you from radiation and alien lazers. You cannot perform a radar search or fire your lazers when the shield is up.

The gyros and shield can be terminated by pressing the clear key.

Radar Search "R"

Pressing the R key will cost ten units of energy and flash the position of the alien on the screen. Make sure the shield is down!

Fire Lazers "L"

Pressing the L key will cost you ten units of energy. The alien will be eliminated if it is within ten units of your ship. If the alien is further than ten units, you will receive a "MISSED" message.

Coordinate Check "C"

Pressing the C key will display the coordinates of each planet. Knowing the position of each planet will be useful in making a landing.

Instructions "I"

Pressing the I key will give you a brief summary of the scenerio. The format of the summary is left to the discretion of the programmer because its length and detail should vary considerably with the amount of memory available and the environment in which the program is being used. The instructions should begin with line 700. The present program initiates a time-delay at this point in the program.

Landing on a Planet

You begin your journey with 200 units each of energy and crew morale. Two hundred units is probably not sufficient to meet the objectives of the mission; therefore, during your journey, it will be necessary to land on a planet where you will recover your 200 units of energy and morale.

In order to successfully land on a planet, you must be within two units of the planet and both the x and y velocities must be less than .2. If you pass within two units of a planet with velocities greater than two, up to ten units of energy will be consumed each time-interval to maintain a cool heat shield.

Landing on the "#" planet after the alien is eliminated will complete the mission.

The Alien

One alien is randomly placed near the center of the universe[1] at the beginning of the mission. The alien moves one unit per time-interval randomly in one of four directions, N, E, S, or W, throughout the universe.

---

[1]The space within the coordinate system defined under Anti-space.

If you are within ten units of the alien and your shield is down you will receive a message, You can locate the alien anywhere in the universe by using a random search.

If you are within ten units of the alien, the alien has a 10% chance of "zapping" you if your shields are down. If you get "zapped" you will lose up to 20 units of energy and up to 20 units of crew morale.

Anti-space

The coordinate system goes from 0 to 127 for x and from 0 to 32 for y. If you travel "out of bounds" you will receive an "ANIT-SPACE" message. Your ship will lose up to ten units of energy and your crew will lose up to ten units of morale each time-interval you are in anti-space.

Black Hole

The black hole is located randomly at the beginning of the mission. If you travel within ten units of the black hole, your ship will lose up to ten units of energy and your crew will lose up to ten units of morale for each time-interval you are in this area.

The shield will not protect the ship against anti-space or the black hole.

Radiation

At the beginning of the mission, one of the planets is randomly selected as "hot". The amount of radiation emitted from this planet can be monitored. You will lose up to R units of energy and R units of morale each time-interval, where R is the amount of radiation hitting the ship. The shield will protect the ship and its crew from radiation.

Motor Temperature

As the motors are firing, the temperature increases. When the temperature is over 20 units, a "TOO HOT" alarm is given. An additional unit of energy is required to cool the hot motors. If the motors are not used, they will cool one unit per time-interval.

Morale

The morale of the crew drops one unit each time-interval.

Miscellaneous Hazards

There are five random events, each with a 1% chance of occurring. They are as follows:

EVENT	RESULT OF OCCURENCE
Meteor Hit	x,y position displaced
Fuel Leak	lose a maximum of 20 units of energy
Crew Ill	lose a maximum of 20 units of morale
Space Storm	ship stops; lose a maximum of 20 units of morale
Heat Problem	temperature climbs a maximum of 20 units

Sample Screen Display

```
        *

              *                  *                    #

           *

                   *

              *                      *


    ▌             *               *


                            *            *

    _ _ _ _ _ _ _ _ _ _ _ _ _ _ _ _ _ _ _ _ _ _ _ _ _ _ _ _

                          *****TOO HOT*****


   VX=0.1          VY=0.3      BLACK HOLE  62      ENERGY  125
     X=1.7           Y=7.7           TEMP  30      MORALE   87
                             RADIATION   1        TIME   94.4
```

STARSHIP ALPHA PROGRAM

Variables

A$	Format for vx,vy; "##.#"
B$	Format for s,y,T; "###.#"
C$	Format for energy, morale, black hole,radiation; "###"
Z$	Input
A,B	Location of black hole
C	Planet with radiation(1-1∅)
D	Shield flag for defense(∅ or 1)
E	East flag(∅ or 1)
F	Energy or fuel(∅ - 2∅∅)
G	Gyro flag(∅ or 1)
H	Temperature or heat
I,J,K	Index variables
L,M	Temporary variables
N	North flag
P	Morale(∅ - 2∅∅)
Q	Distance to alien(200 if no alien)
R	Radiation level
S	South flag
T	Time
U,V	Location of alien
W	West flag
X,Y	Location of ship
VX,VY	X and y velocities
PL	Distance to planet

Program Listing

```
 10  CLS:DEFSTR Z:DEFINTI,J,K:DIML(11):A$="##.#":B$="###.#":C$="###"
 15  X=3:Y=25:SET(3,25):F=200:P=200:T=100
 20  A=30+RND(50):B=RND(32)
 25  U=30+RND(50):V=RND(32):C=RND(10)
 30  PRINT@783,"******";TAB(41)"******";
 35  PRINT@832,"VX=";TAB(11)"VY=";TAB(29)"BLACK HOLE";TAB(52);
     "ENERGY";
 40  PRINT@897,"X=";TAB(12)"Y=";TAB(35)"TEMP";TAB(52)"MORALE";
 45  PRINT@990,"RADIATION";TAB(52)"TIME";:FOR I=704TO767:PRINT@I,".";
     :NEXT
 50  FOR I=1TO10:READ J:PRINT@J,"*";:NEXT:PRINT@242,"#";
 55  DATA70,209,595,401,168,564,93,223,420,543,242
 56  DATA12,3,34,10,38,28,34,19,81,7,104,25
 57  DATA59,3,62,10,73,18,63,25,100,10
 60  Z=INKEY$:IF Z=""THEN170
 65  I=ASC(Z):IF Z="C"THEN GOSUB600
 70  IF Z="I"THEN GOSUB700
 75  IF Z="G"G=1:PRINT@961,"GYROS";
 80  IF Z="S"D=1:PRINT@972,"SHIELD";
 85  IF Z<>"R"OR D=1THEN105
 90  PRINT@793,"RADAR SEARCH";:F=F-10:GOSUB500
 95  IF Q=200PRINT@799,"NO ALIENS";:GOSUB500:GOTO105
100  FOR J=1TO4:PRINT@792,"ALIEN LOCATION";:SET(U,V):GOSUB500:
     RESET(U,V):GOSUB500:NEXT
105  IF Z<>"L"OR D=1THEN125
110  PRINT@794,"FIRE  LAZERS";:GOSUB500:F=F-10
115  IF Q>10PRINT@795,"MISSED";:GOSUB500:GOTO125
120  PRINT@792,"ALIEN ELIMINATED";:Q=200:P=100:GOSUB500
125  IF I=91THEN PRINT@779,CHR$(91);:N=1:S=0
130  IF I=10THEN PRINT@779,CHR$(92);:S=1:N=0
135  IF I=9THEN PRINT@768,CHR$(94);:E=1:W=0
140  IF I=8THEN PRINT@768,CHR$(93);:W=1:E=0
149  REM CLEARS
150  IF I=31PRINT@960,"                    ";:G=0:D=0
155  IF I=13THEN PRINT@768,"              ";:N=0:E=0:S=0:W=0
170  IF G=1THEN L=0ELSE L=1
175  IF N=1THEN VY=VY+10+L*RND(50)
180  IF S=1THEN VY=VY-10-L*RND(50)
185  IF E=1THEN VX=VX+10+L*RND(50)
190  IF W=1THEN VX=VX-10-L*RND(50)
195  I=N+S+E+W+D+G:F=F-I:H=H+I-D-G:IF I=0THEN H=H-1:IF H<0THEN H=0
200  PRINT@836," ";:PRINTUSING A$;VX/100;:PRINT@847," ";
     :PRINTUSING A$;VY/100;
205  PRINT@939," ";:PRINTUSING C$;H;
210  IF ABS(VX)>200OR ABS(VY)>200THEN PRINT@793,"WARP SPEED";
     :GOSUB500:F=F-1
215  IF H>20THEN PRINT@795,"TOO HOT";:GOSUB500:F=F-1
220  L=X+VX/100:M=Y-VY/100
230  IF L<1 OR L>1270R M>330R M<0THEN PRINT@792,"ANTI SPACE";
     :GOSUB500:L=X-VX/100:M=Y+VY/100:F=F-RND(10)
235  RESET(X,Y):X=L:Y=M:SET(X,Y)
240  PRINT@900,"";:PRINTUSING B$;X;:PRINT@911,"";:PRINTUSING B$;32-Y;
245  I=SQR((X-A)↑2+(Y-B)↑2):PRINT@875," ";:PRINTUSING C$;I;
```

```
250    IF I<1ØPRINT@792,"BLACK HOLE";:GOSUB5ØØ:F=F-RND(2Ø):P=P-RND(2Ø)
255    IF Q=2ØØOR D=1THEN 295
260    L=U+4-RND(7):M=V+4-RND(7):IF L<ØOR L>127OR M<ØOR M>32THEN25Ø
265    U=L:V=M:Q=SQR((X-U)↑2+(Y-V)↑2)
270    IF Q>2ØTHEN295
275    PRINT@792,"ALIENS NEAR";:GOSUB5ØØ
280    IF1Ø<RND(1ØØ)THEN295
285    PRINT@79Ø,"ALIENS ZAPPED YOU";:GOSUB5ØØ:F=F-RND(2Ø):P=P-RND(2Ø)
295    IF D=1THEN R=Ø:GOTO325
300    RESTORE:FOR I=1TO1Ø:READ J:NEXT
305    FOR I=1TO C:READ J,K:NEXT
310    R=SQR((X-J)↑2+(Y-K)↑2)
315    R=(1/R)↑2*5ØØØ
320    F=F-RND(R):P=P-RND(R)
325    PRINT@1ØØ3," ";:PRINTUSING C$;R;
330    RESTORE:FOR I=1TO11:READ J:NEXT
335    FOR PL=1TO11:READ J,K:L=SQR((X-J)↑2+(Y-K)↑2)
400    IF L>2 OR ABS( VX)>2ØOR ABS(VY) >2ØTHEN416
405    IF L<2AND ABS( VX)<2ØAND ABS(VY)<2ØPRINT@792,"SOFT LANDING";:
       GOSUB5ØØ:F=2ØØ:P=2ØØ
410    IF PL=11AND Q=2ØØTHEN PRINT@79Ø,"MISSION COMPLETED";:GOSUB5ØØ:
       GOTO41Ø
415    IF L<2AND( ABS(VX)>2ØOR ABS(VY)) >2ØPRINT@792,"IN ATMOSPHERE ";:
       GOSUB5ØØ:H=H+RND(1Ø)
416    IF L>1AND L<6THEN RESTORE:FOR I=1TO1Ø:READ J:PRINT@J,"*";:NEXT:
       PRINT@242,"#"
418    NEXTPL
420    IF T<=ØTHEN PRINT@1Ø18,"ØØØ";: T=Ø:PRINT@794,"OUT OF TIME";:
       GOSUB 5ØØ:GOTO42Ø
425    T=T-.1:P=P-1:PRINT@1Ø17," ";:PRINTUSINGB$;T;
430    IF F<=ØPRINT@892,"ØØØ";:PRINT@793,"OUT OF ENERGY";:GOSUB5ØØ
       :GOTO43Ø
435    PRINT@891," ";:PRINTUSINGC$;F;
440    IF P<=ØPRINT@956,"ØØØ";:PRINT@795,"MUTINY!!";:GOSUB5ØØ:GOTO44Ø
445    PRINT@955," ";:PRINTUSINGC$;P;
450    GOSUB8ØØ
460    GOTO6Ø
500    FOR I=1TO8ØØ:NEXT:PRINT@79Ø,"                   ";:RETURN
600    RESTORE:FOR I=1TO11:READ L(I):NEXT
610    FOR I=1TO11:READ J,K
620    PRINT@L(I)+1,J;",";32-K;:NEXT
630    FOR I=1TO1ØØØ:NEXT
640    FOR I=1TO11:PRINT@L(I)+1,"          ";:NEXT:RETURN
700    FOR I=1TO2ØØØ:NEXT:GOSUB5ØØ:RETURN
800    ONRND(1ØØ)GOSUB81Ø,82Ø,83Ø,84Ø,85Ø
805    RETURN
810    PRINT@792,"METEOR HIT";:GOSUB7ØØ
815    L=X+6-RND(11):M=Y+6-RND(11)
817    IF L<ØORL>127OR M<ØOR M>32THEN RETURN
818    RESET(X,Y):X=L:Y=M:SET(X,Y):RETURN
820    PRINT@792,"FUEL LEAK";:GOSUB7ØØ:F=F-RND(2Ø):RETURN
830    PRINT@794,"CREW ILL";:GOSUB7ØØ:P=P-RND(2Ø):RETURN
840    PRINT@792,"SPACE STORM";:GOSUB7ØØ:VX=Ø:VY=Ø:P=P+RND(1Ø):RETURN
850    PRINT@792,"HEAT PROBLEM";:GOSUB7ØØ:H=H+1Ø:RETURN
```

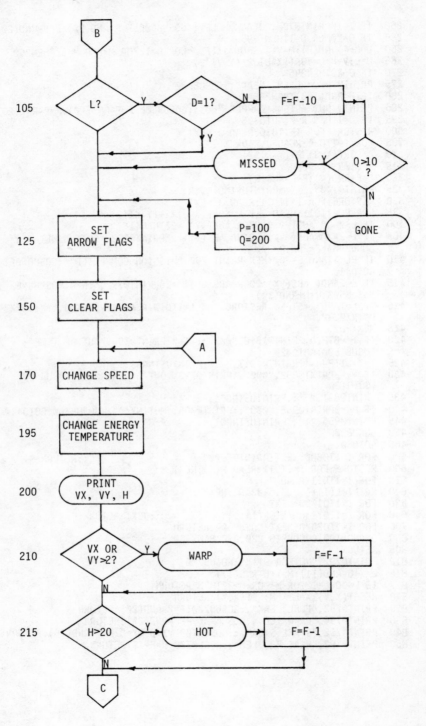

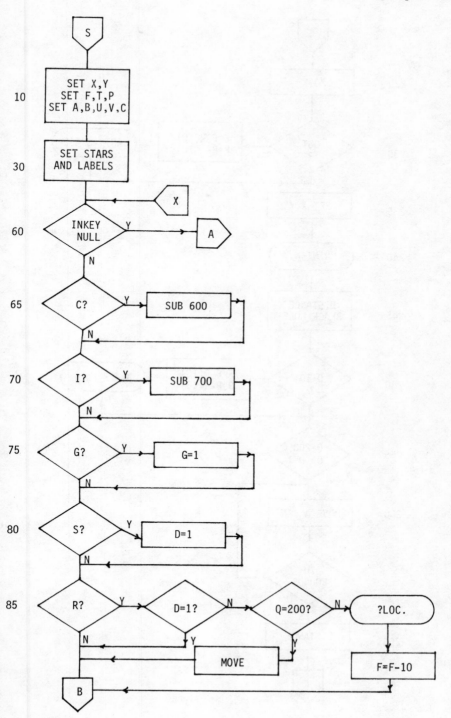

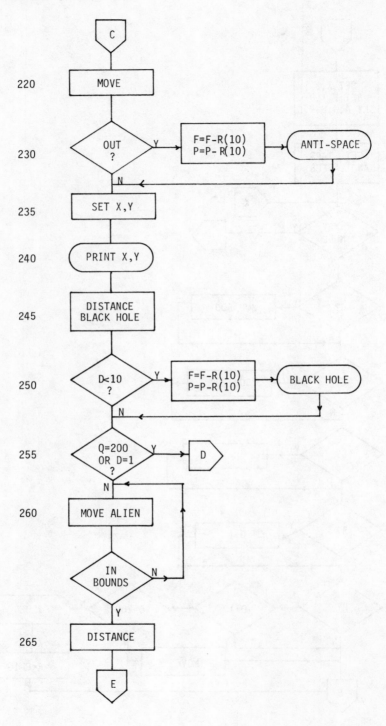

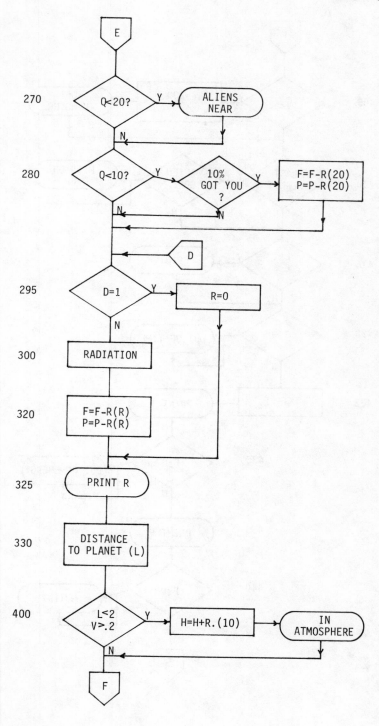

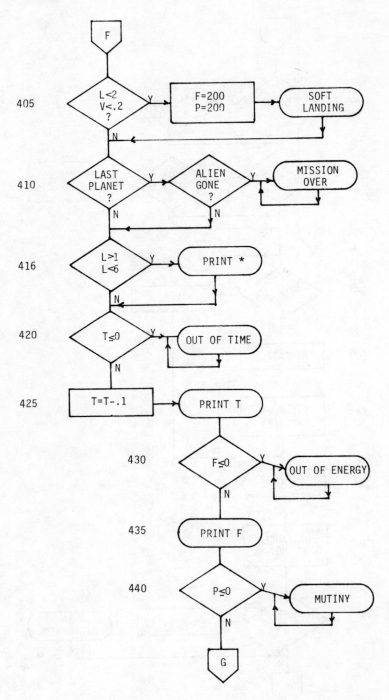

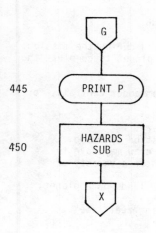

SUBROUTINES

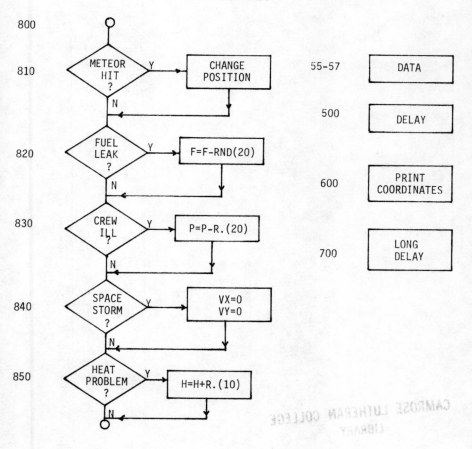

STARSHIP ALPHA MODIFICATIONS

1. More than one alien spaceship is encountered during the mission.
2. Starship Alpha must land on more than one planet to complete the mission.
3. The number of hazards is increased.
4. Increase the number of devices that the commander controls, for example, offensive and defensive weapons.
5. Aliens attack the spaceship.
6. Devices break and a repair time is necessary.
7. Gravitational effects from the planets must be overcome.
8. When the spaceship lands on a planet, the crew may have to battle monsters, hunt for fuel, and encounter a variety of adventures.
9. When the spaceship is close to a planet or lands on a planet, this area is magnified on the video display.
10. Competition with another computer system in "real time".

FOREST FIRE

Scenario

A lightening storm has ignited fires in a forest. Your task is to put out the fires and save as many trees as possible. The forest is divided into 81 sectors formed by a 9X9 grid. Each sector is identified by the number of its row and column. The symbol, ".", represents woods, an "*" represents fire, and a blank space represents burnt out woods.

The chance of an existing fire spreading to adjacent wooded areas is 70%. Fires last for nine turns before burning out.

You have two weapons with which to fight the fire. You can drop chemicals that are designed to extinguish the fires in a specified sector. The chance that the drop will affect the fires in this sector and its eight adjacent sectors is 50%. For example, if there are six fires burning in a nine-square area, approximately three will be affected by the chemicals. The effect of chemicals is to reduce the number of turns before the fire burns out by three. Since a fire lasts only nine turns, three successful chemical hits will be needed to extinguish a fire. If the fire has been burning for six turns, then one hit will suffice.

The second weapon available to you is a backfire. To start a backfire, you must respond to the row input with a zero. You will then be asked for a backfire row and column. The sector in which a backfire is started must be wooded. This backfire will not spread and will burn out in the next turn, forming a barrier against the spread of fire.

Your rating will be the number of trees remaining after all the fires are out, plus 30.

Sample Run

```
               #1                              #4                              #12
    1 2 3 4 5 6 7 8 9               1 2 3 4 5 6 7 8 9               1 2 3 4 5 6 7 8 9
1   . . . . . . . . .           1   . . . . . . . . .           1   . . . * * . . . *
2   . . . . . . . . .           2   . . . . . . . . .           2   . . . . * * . . .
3   . . . . . . . . .           3   . . . . . . . * .           3   . . . . . . . . .
4   . . . . . . . * .           4   . . . . . . * . .           4   . . . . . . . . .
5   . . . . . . . * .           5   . * . . . * * .             5   . * . . . . . . .
6   . . . * . . . . .           6   . . * . . * * .             6   . . . . . . . . .
7   . . . . . . . . .           7   . * . . . . . . .           7   . . . . . . . * .
8   . . . . . . . . .           8   . . . . . . . . .           8   . . . . . . * . .
9   . . . . . . . . .           9   . . . . . . . . .           9   . . . * . . * . .

ROW?  0                         ROW?  6                         ROW?  8
BACKFIRE ROW?  4                COLUMN?  3                      COLUMN?  7
BACKFIRE COLUMN?  7
```

```
               #2
    1 2 3 4 5 6 7 8 9
1   . . . . . . . . .
2   . . . . . . . . .
3   . . . . . . . . .
4   . . . . . . * * .
5   . . . . . . . * .
6   . . . * . . . . .
7   . * . . . . . . .
8   . . . . . . . . .
9   . . . . . . . . .

ROW?  0                                                         #16
BACKFIRE ROW?  5                                    1 2 3 4 5 6 7 8 9
BACKFIRE COLUMN?  7                             1   . . . . * . .
                                                2   . . . . . . .
                                                3   . . . . . . .
                               #11              4   . . . . . . .
                    1 2 3 4 5 6 7 8 9           5   . . . . . . .
                1   . . . * * . . * *           6   . . . . * . .
                2   . . . * * * . .             7   . . . . . . .
               #3                               8   . . . . . . .
    1 2 3 4 5 6 7 8 9           3   . . . . . . .   9   . . . . . . .
1   . . . . . . . . .           4   . . . . . . . . .
2   . . . . . . . . .           5   . * . . . . .   ROW?  6
3   . . . . . . . . *           6   * . . . . . .   COLUMN?  6
4   . . . . . . . * .           7   . * . . . * .
5   . . * . . . * * .           8   . . . . . . * .
6   . . . * . . . * .           9   . . * . . * . .
7   . . * . . . . . .
8   . . . . . . . . .           ROW?  6                         YOUR RATING IS 69.
9   . . . . . . . . .           COLUMN?  2                      PLAY AGAIN?

ROW?  0
BACKFIRE ROW?  6
BACKFIRE COLUMN?  7
```

FOREST FIRE FLOWCHART

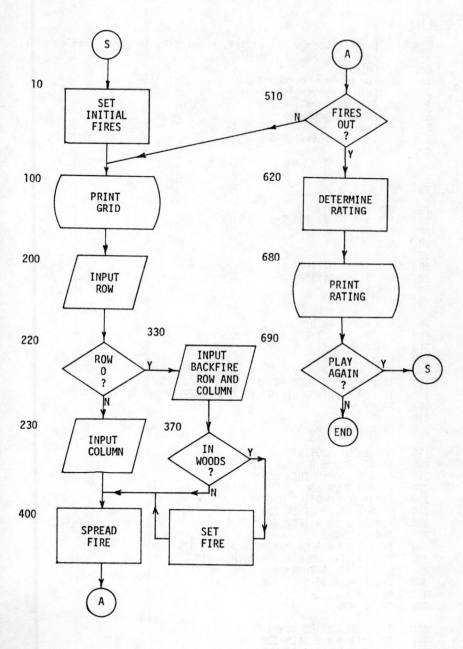

FOREST FIRE PROGRAM

Variables

L(R,C)	Burnt woods: 0, fire: 1-9, woods: 10, temporary variable: 11
R	Row
C	Column
I	Row number increment
J	Column number increment
A	Adjacent row
B	Adjacent column
F	Count
T	Temporary variable
R	Rating

Listing

```
10      DIM L(9,9)
20      FOR R=1 TO 9: FOR C=1 TO 9
30      L(R,C)=10
40      NEXT C,R
50      FOR I=1 TO 3
60      R=INT(9*RND(1)+1)
70      C=INT(9*RND(1)+1)
80      L(R,C)=9
90      NEXT I

95      REM PRINT GRID
100     PRINT "    1 2 3 4 5 6 7 8 9"
110     FOR R=1 TO 9
120     PRINT R; " ";
130     FOR C=1 TO 9
140     IF L(R,C)=10 THEN PRINT ".";: GO TO 170
150     IF L(R,C)>0 AND L(R,C)<10 THEN PRINT "*";: GO TO 170
160     PRINT " ";
170     NEXT C
180     PRINT: NEXT R

195     REM INPUT ROUTINE
200     INPUT "ROW"; R
210     IF R<0 OR R>9 THEN 200
220     IF R=0 THEN 330
230     INPUT "COLUMN"; C
240     IF C<1 OR C>9 THEN 230
250     FOR I=-1 TO 1: FOR J=-1 TO 1
260     A=R+I: B=C+J
270     IF A<1 OR A>9 OR B<1 OR B>9 THEN 310
280     IF L(A,B)<1 OR L(A,B)=10 THEN 310
290     IF RND(1)>.5 THEN 310
300     L(A,B)=L(A,B)-3
310     NEXT J,I
320     GO TO 400

330     INPUT "BACKFIRE ROW"; R
340     IF R<1 OR R>9 THEN 330
350     INPUT "BACKFIRE COLUMN"; C
360     IF C<1 OR C>9 THEN 350
```

```
370    IF L(R,C)=10 THEN L(R,C)=2

395    REM SPREAD FIRE
400    FOR R=1 TO 9: FOR C=1 TO 9
410    IF L(R,C)<1 OR L(R,C)>9 THEN 500
420    IF L(R,C)<3 THEN 500
430    I=INT(3*RND(1)-1)
440    J=INT(3*RND(1)-1)
450    A=R+I: B=C+J
460    IF A<1 OR A>9 OR B<1 OR B>9 THEN 500
470    IF L(A,B)<>10 THEN 500
480    IF RND(1)<.3 THEN 500
490    L(A,B)=11
500    NEXT C,R

505    REM BURN FIRE AND COUNT
510    F=0
520    FOR R=1 TO 9
530    FOR C=1 TO 9
540    T=L(R,C)
550    IF T=11 THEN T=9
560    IF T>0 AND T<10 THEN T=T-1: F=F+1
570    L(R,C)=T
580    NEXT C,R
590    IF F<1 THEN 620
600    GO TO 100

615    REM COUNT WOODS RATING
620    C=0
630    FOR R=1 TO 9: FOR C=1 TO 9
640    IF L(R,C)=10 THEN W=W+1
650    NEXT C,R
660    R=W+30
670    IF R>100 THEN R=100
680    PRINT "YOUR RATING IS"; R; "."
690    INPUT "PLAY AGAIN"; Y$
700    IF Y$="Y" THEN RUN
710    END
```

FOREST FIRE MODIFICATIONS

Minor

1. Number of beginning fires -- line 50
2. Location of beginning fires -- lines 60, 70
3. Probability of putting out fire -- line 290
4. Amount fire burns out each turn -- line 300
5. Size of backfire -- line 370
6. Probability of spread -- line 480
7. Size of spread fires -- line 550
8. Rating scale - lines 660, 670

Major

1. Change grid size.
2. Randomly choose location of beginning fires.
3. Add time to move from one place to another.
4. Have wind speed and direction affect the spread of the fire.
5. Include barriors such as lakes and roads.
6. Have some of the sectors burn faster than others.

NAUTICAL NAVIGATION

Scenario

Your task is to navigate a sailboat that has an electronic direction finder to three different islands in the South Pacific. You do not have to dock at the islands, but only come close enough to make a visual sighting. The minimum sighting distance will vary from five to ten miles, depending upon weather conditions.

The islands are located at coordinates (200,300), (600,300), and (300,100). Your starting location will be approximately (200,200). You will need graph paper and an inexpensive protractor and ruler in order to plot your course.

Each turn you will receive information about your bearings in degrees from each of the three islands. For convenience, you will also receive the bearings from the ship to each of the islands. The example below shows how the bearings are determined. If you know the bearing from two of the three islands, you can locate the ship; however, there are some random errors in the readings, so it might be wise to use the readings from all three islands.

Bearing from island #1: 317°; bearing to island #1: 138°.
Bearing from island #2: 230°; bearing to island #2: 50°.

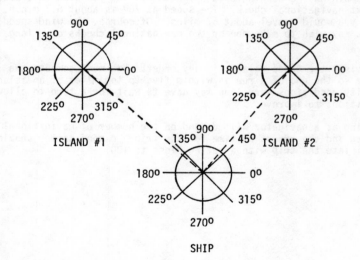

SHIP

After you locate your position, you must determine your heading and the length of time you wish to remain on this course. You can use the heading from the ship to the island of your destination to determine the ship's heading. Since you are in a sailboat, your speed will depend on your direction with respect to an easterly wind. In order to make any progress toward the East, you must tack at either 45° or 315°. The speed of the sailboat as a function of its direction is shown in the graph below.

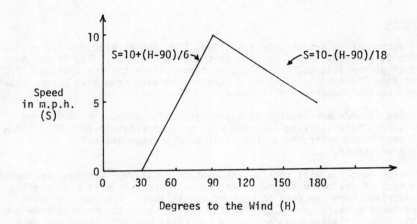

$$S=10+(H-90)/6$$
$$S=10-(H-90)/18$$

Speed in m.p.h. (S)

Degrees to the Wind (H)

The fastest speed of ten miles per hour is acheived when the boat is perpendicular to the wind -- heading either directly north (90^0) or south (270^0). When the boat is running with the wind directly behind it, its speed is about half the maximum speed or five m.p.h.

Once you determine the heading, you must determine the length of time you wish to remain on the heading or the length of time you wish to travel before the next navigational check. The speed at 70^0 is about 6.7 m.p.h. In ten hours, you would travel about 67 miles. Of course, the wind speed varies; so you may wish to make one or two navigational checks on a long run.

You can visit the three islands in any order. You must compute the angle and time so the end of a run is within five to ten miles of an island. Since visibility conditions vary, you may have to wait for a turn to allow sighting conditions to improve.

Your rating as a navigator will depend on the number of navigational checks required and the amount of time for the trip. A good sailor should be able to complete the trip with a rating close to 100.

Sample Run

NAVIGATION CHECK 1
BEARING FROM 1: 279   TO: 99
BEARING FROM 2: 197   TO: 17
BEARING FROM 3: 136   TO: 316
ELAPSED TIME 0
HEADING? 99
TIME? 33

NAVIGATION CHECK 2
BEARING FROM 1 : 97   TO: 277
BEARING FROM 2: 158   TO: 338
BEARING FROM 3: 108   TO: 288
ELAPSED TIME 32.9694
HEADING? 277
TIME? 20

NAVIGATION CHECK 3
VISITED 1
BEARING FROM 1: 84   TO: 264
BEARING FROM 2: 179   TO: 359
BEARING FROM 3: 115   TO: 295
ELAPSED TIME 52.9576
HEADING? 295
TIME? 30

NAVIGATION CHECK 4
VISITED 1
BEARING FROM 1: 296   TO: 116
BEARING FROM 2: 201   TO: 21
BEARING FROM 3: 117   TO: 297
ELAPSED TIME 82.9246
HEADING? 297
TIME? 10

NAVIGATION CHECK 5
VISITED 1
BEARING FROM 1: 296   TO: 116
BEARING FROM 2 : 209   TO: 29
BEARING FROM 3: 114   TO: 294
ELAPSED TIME 92.8834
HEADING? 294
TIME? 3

NAVIGATION CHECK 6
VISITED 1
VISITED 3
BEARING FROM 1: 296   TO: 116
BEARING FROM 2: 212   TO: 32
BEARING FROM 3: 119   TO: 299
ELAPSED TIME 95.8568
HEADING? 60
TIME? 120

NAVIGATION CHECK 7
VISITED 1
VISITED 3
BEARING FROM 1: 35   TO: 215
BEARING FROM 2: 92   TO: 272
BEARING FROM 3: 58   TO: 238
ELAPSED TIME 215.833
HEADING? 272
TIME? 28

TRIP COMPLETED IN 243.859 HOURS
NUMBER OF NAVIGATIONAL CHECKS 7
YOUR RATING IS 66
PLAY AGAIN?

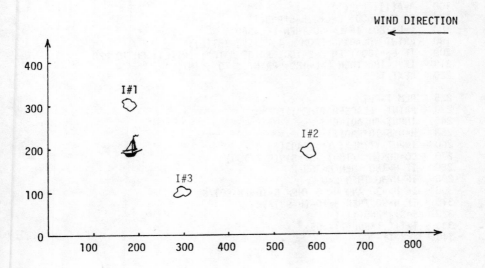

WIND DIRECTION

NAUTICAL NAVIGATION PROGRAM

Variables

D(3)	Set to 1 if arrived at destination
A(3),B(3)	Coordinates of islands
X,Y	Coordinates of ship
E	Total elapsed time
C	Number of navigational checks
L	Angle bearing from island
H	Heading of ship
T	Time for one leg of trip
A,B	Temporary variables
Y$	Play again

Listing

```
5       REM PLACE ISLANDS AND SHIP
10      DIM A(3), B(3), D(3)
20      E=0: P=3.14159
30      FOR I=1 TO 3
40      READ A,B
50      A(I)=10*A: B(I)=10*B
60      D(I)=0
70      NEXT I
80      DATA 20,30,60,20,30,10
90      X=175+50*RND(1): Y=175+50*RND(1)

95      REM START MAIN LOOP
100     FOR C=1 TO 100
110     PRINT "NAVIGATION CHECK"; C
120     FOR I=1 TO 3
130     IF D(I)=1 THEN PRINT "VISITED"; I
140     NEXT I

150     FOR I=1 TO 3
160     A=A(I): B=B(I)
170     GO SUB 600: L=L+2.5-5*RND(1)
180     L=L+180: IF L>360 THEN L=L-360
190     PRINT "BEARING FROM"; I; "IS"; INT(L);
200     IF L>=180 THEN L=L-180: PRINT " TO"; INT(L): GO TO 220
210     IF L<180 THEN L=L+180: PRINT " TO"; INT(L)
220     NEXT I

225     REM INPUT
230     PRINT "ELAPSED TIME"; E
240     INPUT "HEADING"; H
250     H=H+5-10*RND(1)
260     INPUT "TIME"; T: T=ABS(T)
270     CO=COS(H*P/180): SI=SIN(H*P/180)
280     IF H>180 THEN H=360-H
290     IF H<30 THEN S=0
300     IF H>=30 AND H<90 THEN S=10+(H-90)/6
310     IF H>90 THEN S=10-(H-90)/18
320     S=S+2*RND(1)-1
330     T=T+(.1*RND(1)-.05)
340     X=X+T*S*CO
```

```
350    Y=Y+T*S*SI
360    E=E+T

400    FOR I = 1 TO 3
410    D=SQR((X-A(I))↑2+(Y-B(I))↑2)
420    IF D<5+10*RND(1) THEN D(I)=1
430    NEXT I
440    IF D(1)+D(2)+D(3)=3 THEN GO TO 500
450    NEXT C
460    PRINT "EXCEED NAVIGATION CHECK": GO TO 530
500    PRINT "TRIP COMPLETED IN"; E; "HOURS."
510    PRINT "NUMBER OF NAVIGATION CHECKS IS"; C; "."
520    PRINT "YOUR RATING IS"; 170-(INT(E+10*C/3))
530    INPUT "PLAY AGAIN"; Y$
540    IF Y$="Y" THEN RUN
550    END

600    IF X=A AND Y>B THEN L=270: RETURN
610    IF X=A AND Y<B THEN L=90: RETURN
620    N=ABS(Y-B)/ABS(X-A)
630    L=ATN(N): L=180*L/P
640    IF X>A AND Y>=B THEN L=L+180
650    IF X<A AND Y>B THEN L=360-L
660    IF X>A AND Y<B THEN L=180-L
670    RETURN
```

NAUTICAL NAVIGATION MODIFICATIONS

Minor

1. Location of islands -- line 80
2. Starting place of ship -- line 90
3. Error in angle -- line 170
4. Input error -- line 250
5. Speed error -- line 320
6. Time error -- line 330
7. Sighting criteria -- line 420
8. Rating -- line 520

Major

1. Change number of islands.
2. Have storms.
3. Have wind direction change.

NAUTICAL NAVIGATION FLOWCHART

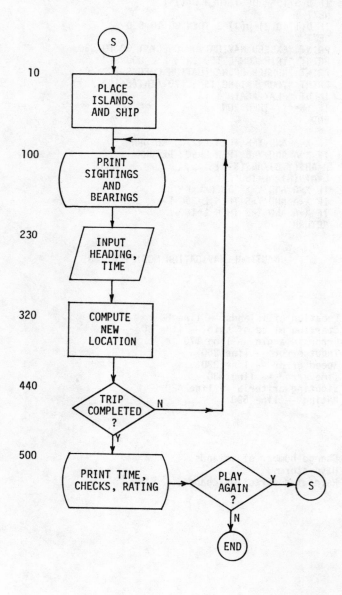

BUSINESS MANAGEMENT

Scenario

In this simulation you manage a small factory that produces three different kinds of products (P1 - P3). Three different kinds of raw materials (R1 - R3) are required to produce the products. Each product requires exactly two raw materials with a different subscript. For example, to manufacture one unit of P2, you would need a unit of R1 and a unit of R3. To manufacture one unit of P3, you would need a unit of R1 and R2.

The cost of raw materials varies from $10 to $20 per unit. It costs from $1 to $9 per unit to manufacture a product from raw materials. The selling price of each finished product varies from $50 to $90 per unit. Prices of raw materials and manufacturing costs will vary by not more than $2 per turn. Prices of finished products will vary by not more than $5 per turn.

You will receive a data report at the beginning of each turn. This report will give you the number of units you have on hand, available cash, and the manufacturing costs. You can buy, manufacture, or sell each turn. In order to manufacture a given product, you must have enough of the correct kind of materials on hand.

After twelve turns (months), the materials and/or products that you have on hand will be automatically sold at the current prices and your profit will be computed.

Sample Run

```
ITEM        MATERIALS        PRODUCTS
1           $0-$16           $0-$72
2           $0-$15           $0-$72
3           $0-$17           $0-$73
MONTH 0   YOU HAVE $500
MANUFACTURING COSTS ARE $2
TRANSACTION O,B,M,S?  B
AMOUNT OF MATERIALS?  10
ITEM#?  2


ITEM        MATERIALS        PRODUCTS
1           $0-$16           $0-$67
2           $10-$16          $0-$71
3           $0-$16           $0-$73
MONTH 1   YOU HAVE $350
MANUFACTURING COSTS ARE $1
TRANSACTION O,B,M,S?  B
AMOUNT OF MATERIALS?  10
ITEM#?  1
```

```
ITEM        MATERIALS        PRODUCTS
1           $10-$18          $0-$63
2           $10-$17          $0-$70
3           $0-$18           $0-$68
MONTH 2   YOU HAVE $190
MANUFACTURING COSTS ARE $2
TRANSACTION O,B,M,S?   M
MANUFACTURE AMOUNT?   10
ITEM#?   3
```

```
ITEM        MATERIALS        PRODUCTS
1           $0-$19           $0-$67
2           $0-$15           $0-$72
3           $0-$18           $10-$73
MONTH 3   YOU HAVE $170
MANUFACTURING COSTS ARE $2
TRANSACTION O,B,M,S?   S
AMOUNT TO SELL?   10
ITEM#?   3
```

```
ITEM        MATERIALS        PRODUCTS
1           $0-$17           $0-$72
2           $0-$17           $0-$76
3           $0-$18           $0-$77
MONTH 4   YOU HAVE $900
MANUFACTURING COSTS ARE $3
TRANSACTION O,B,M,S?
```

```
                  .
                  .
                  .
```

```
ITEM        MATERIALS        PRODUCTS
1           $0-$18           $0-$71
2           $0-$12           $0-$62
3           $0-$10           $0-$68
MONTH 12   YOU HAVE $2380
MANUFACTURING COSTS ARE $8
TRANSACTION O,B,M,S?   O
END OF YEAR
YOUR PROFIT IS 1880.
PLAY AGAIN?
```

BUSINESS MANAGEMENT FLOWCHART

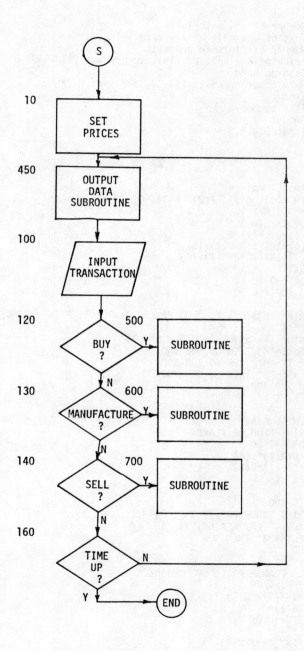

BUSINESS MANAGEMENT PROGRAM

Variables

R(I)	Number of raw materials
C(I)	Cost of one unit of raw material
F(I)	Number of finished products
P(I)	Price of one unit of finished product ($50-$90)
C	Cash on hand
M	Manufacturing costs ($1-$9) per unit
T	Time
N	Item number
A	Amount
T$	Input O,B,M,S

Listing

```
5       REM SET PRICES
10      DIM R(3), C(3), F(3), P(3)
20      C=500: M=2
30      FOR I=1 TO 3
40      R(I)=0: F(I)=0
50      C(I)=INT(3*RND(1)+15)
60      P(I)=INT(10*RND(1)+70)
70      NEXT I
80      FOR T=0 TO 12
90      GO SUB 450

100     PRINT "MONTH"; T; "YOU HAVE"; C: PRINT: PRINT "MANUFACTURING
        COSTS ARE $"; M
110     INPUT "TRANSACTION O,B,M,S"; T$
120     IF T$="B" THEN GO SUB 500
130     IF T$="M" THEN GO SUB 600
140     IF T$="S" THEN GO SUB 700
150     GO SUB 300
160     NEXT T

165     REM SUMMARY
170     PRINT "END OF YEAR"
180     FOR I=1 TO 3
190     C=C+R(I)*C(I)
200     C=C+F(I)*P(I)
210     NEXT I

220     C=C-500
230     PRINT "YOUR PROFIT IS"; C; "."
240     INPUT "PLAY AGAIN"; Y$
250     IF Y$="Y" THEN RUN
260     END

295     REM CHANGE PRICE SUBROUTINE
300     FOR I=1 TO 3
310     J=INT(5*RND(1)-2)
320     J=C(I)+J
330     IF J<10 OR J>20 THEN 310
340     C(I)=J
350     J=INT(11*RND(1)-5)
360     J=P(I)+J
```

```
370    IF J<50 OR J>90 THEN 350
380    P(I)=J
390    NEXT I

400    J=INT(5+RND(1)-2)
410    J=M+J
420    IF J<1 OR J>9 THEN 400
430    M=J
440    RETURN

445    REM OUTPUT DATA
450    PRINT "ITEM      MATERIALS      PRODUCT": PRINT
460    FOR I=1 TO 3
470    PRINT I; "    "; R(I); " $"; C(I); "    "; F(I); " $"; P(I):PRINT
480    NEXT I
490    RETURN

495    REM BUY MATERIALS
500    INPUT "AMOUNT OF MATERIALS"; A
510    INPUT "ITEM#"; N
520    IF N<1 OR N>3 THEN PRINT "ERROR": RETURN
530    C=C-A*C(N)
540    IF C<0 THEN 570
550    R(N)=R(N)+A
560    RETURN
570    C=C+A*C(N)
580    PRINT "INSUFFICIENT FUNDS"
590    RETURN

595    REM MANUFACTURE
600    INPUT "MANUFACTURE AMOUNT"; A: INPUT "ITEM#"; N
610    IF N<0 OR N>3 THEN PRINT "ERROR": RETURN
620    C=C-A*M
630    IF C<0 THEN PRINT "INSUFFICIENT FUNDS": C=C+A*M: RETURN

640    FOR I=1 TO 3
650    IF I=N THEN 680
660    R(I)=R(I)-A
670    IF R(I)<0 THEN PRINT "MATERIALS GONE": R(I)=R(I)+A: C=C+A*M:
       RETURN
680    NEXT I: F(N)=F(N)+A: RETURN

695    REM SELL
700    INPUT "AMOUNT TO SELL"; A: INPUT "ITEM#"; N
710    IF N<0 OR N>3 THEN PRINT "ERROR": RETURN
720    F(N)=F(N)-A
730    IF F(N)<0 THEN 760
740    C=C+A*P(N)
750    RETURN
760    F(N)=F(N)+A
770    PRINT "PRODUCTS GONE"
780    RETURN
```

BUSINESS MANAGEMENT MODIFICATIONS

Minor

1. Starting amounts -- lines 20, 50, 60
2. Number of turns -- line 80
3. Amount raw materials vary -- line 310
4. Range of raw materials -- line 330
5. Amount products vary -- line 350
6. Range of products -- line 370
7. Amount manufacturing costs vary -- line 400
8. Range of manufacturing costs -- line 420

Major

1. Increase number of raw materials and finished products.
2. Have a storage fee.
3. When you buy, prices increase.
4. When you sell, prices decrease.
5. Borrow money with interest.
6. Add random events, such as strikes, shortage of materials, fires, no demand.
7. Provide names for raw materials and products.

RARE BIRDS

Scenario

In this simulation you attempt to identify as many birds as possible in a ten hour period. First, you must choose a place to watch birds. It must be in the swamp (S), the water (W), the desert (D), or the forest (F). Then you must choose a time of day -- morning (M), or evening (E). Finally, you must choose to look up in the sky -- high (H) or on the ground -- low (L). There are sixteen different birds that can be identified. The birds are classified as small or big, yellow or blue, shortbeaked or long beaked, and female or male.

After you have selected a place to watch birds, you will receive one clue about the bird and the length of time it took you to spot it. If no bird is spotted in a two-hour period, you may try a new place. After receiving your clue, you then have an opportunity to identify the bird. You should refer to the bird watching chart to determine where the birds are seen and their specific characteristics. The birds with the larger numbers are observed more frequently.

If your first identification is not correct, you will have an opportunity to try again. Each time you try, however, one point will be subtracted from your final rating. If you identify a bird that you have identified correctly before, you will be notified of the fact and may try a new place. Your final rating is determined by multiplying ten times the number of birds identified and subtracting one for each incorrect identification.

Sample Run

```
PLACE S,W,D,F?  S
WHEN M,E?  E
WHERE H,L?  L
THE BIRD IS YELLOW
TIME LAPSE:  1.28
TOTAL TIME:  1.28
IDENTIFY 1-16?  12

NOT CORRECT IDENTIFICATION
IDENTIFY 1-16?  12
A NEW ONE!

PLACE S,W,D,F?  W
WHEN M,E?  E
WHERE H,L?  H
THE BIRD IS BIG
TIME LAPSE:  .18
TOTAL TIME:  1.46
IDENTIFY 1-16?  11

NOT CORRECT IDENTIFICATION
IDENTIFY 1-16?  9
A NEW ONE!
  .
  .
  .

PLACE S,W,D,F?  S
WHEN M,E?  E
WHERE H,L?  L
NO SIGHTINGS
  .
  .
  .

TIME UP
YOU SAW BIRD#  1
               6
               9
               12
               15
               16
YOUR RATING IS  57
PLAY AGAIN?
```

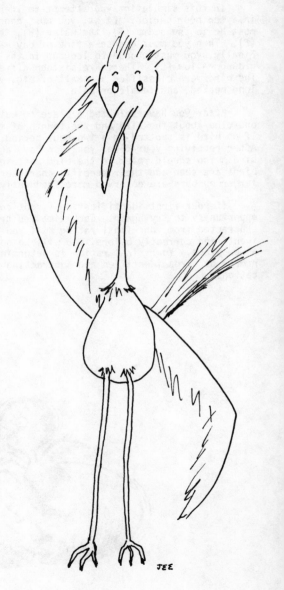

RARE BIRDS FLOWCHART

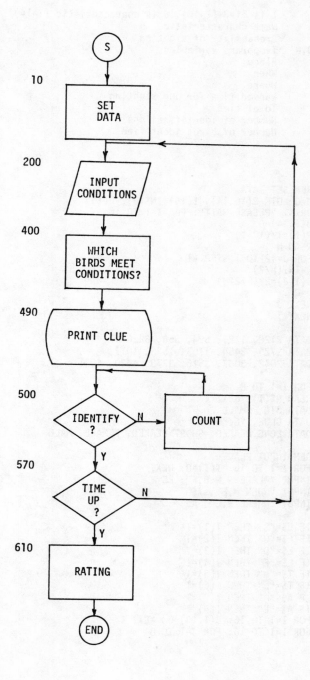

Variables

B(I,J)	I is bird (1-16); J is characteristic (1-14)
N$(I)	Name characteristic
P(I)	Probability of sighting
K,I,J,Q,N	Temporary variables
L$	Place
T$	When
A$	Where
I	Lapsed time for one sighting
H	Total time
B_1	Number of identifications
C_1	Number of birds identified

Listing

```
5      REM SET DATA
10     H=0: DIM B(16,14), I(16), N$(8), P(16)
20     PRINT "PLEASE WAIT": FOR I=1 TO 16
30     B(I,14)=0
40     P(I)=1/(17-I)
50     READ N
60     FOR J=12 TO 1 STEP -1
70     Q=INT(N/2)
80     B(I,J)=2*(N/2-Q)
90     N=Q
100    NEXT J
110    NEXT I

120    DATA 2128, 1121, 594, 355, 3220
130    DATA 2725, 2454, 1703, 1528, 1017
140    DATA 2042, 3067, 3516, 3773, 4030, 4031

150    FOR I=1 TO 8
160    READ N$(I): NEXT I
170    DATA BIG, SMALL
180    DATA BLUE, YELLOW
190    DATA LONG BEAKED, SHORT BEAKED, FEMALE, MALE

195    REM INPUT PLACE
200    FOR I=1 TO 16: I(I)=0: NEXT
210    INPUT "PLACE S,W,D,F"; L$
220    INPUT "WHEN M,E"; T$
230    INPUT "WHERE H,L"; A$

260    IF L$="S" THEN I(1)=1
270    IF L$="W" THEN I(2)=1
280    IF L$="D" THEN I(3)=1
290    IF L$="F" THEN I(4)=1
300    IF T$="M" THEN I(5)=1
310    IF T$="E" THEN I(6)=1
320    IF A$="H" THEN I(7)=1
330    IF A$="L" THEN I(8)=1
340    FOR I=1 TO 16: B(I,13)=0: NEXT I
350    FOR I=1 TO 16: FOR J=1 TO 8
```

```
360    IF B(I,J)<>I(J) AND B(I,J)=0 THEN 390
370    NEXT J
380    B(I,13)=1
390    NEXT I

395    REM FIND BIRDS
400    FOR I=1 TO 2 STEP .02
410    J=INT(16*RND(1)+1)
420    IF B(J,13)<>1 THEN 440
430    IF RND(1)<P(J) THEN 460
440    NEXT I
450    PRINT "NO SIGHTINGS": H=H+I: GO TO 200
460    H=H+I
470    K=INT(4*RND(1)+1)
480    N=B(J,K+8)
490    PRINT "THE BIRD IS"; N$(2*K-N): PRINT "TIME LAPSE:"; I: PRINT
       "TOTAL TIME:"; H

495    REM INPUT ID
500    INPUT "IDENTIFY 1-16"; I
510    IF I=J THEN 530
520    PRINT "NOT CORRECT IDENTIFICATION": C1=C1+1: GO TO 500
530    IF B(J,14)=1 THEN PRINT "ALREADY SPOTTED": GO TO 550
540    PRINT "A NEW ONE!": B(J,14)=1
550    IF H>10 THEN 570
560    GO TO 200

570    PRINT "TIME UP"
580    FOR I=1 TO 16
590    IF B(I,14)=1 THEN PRINT "YOU SAW BIRD #"; I: B1=B1+1
600    NEXT I
610    PRINT "YOUR RATING IS"; 10*B1-C1; "."
620    INPUT "PLAY AGAIN"; Y$
630    IF Y$="Y" THEN RUN
640    END
```

RARE BIRDS MODIFICATIONS

Minor

1. Probability of sighting -- line 40
2. Time interval per turn -- line 400
3. Total time -- line 550
4. Rating formula -- line 610

Major

1. Increase number of birds.
2. Increase characteristics of birds.
3. Allow a bird to be identified more than once.
4. Have some extremely rare birds.

Note: The birds' characteristics are stored in decimal format in state-
      ments 120, 130, and 140. Statements 50-100 convert the decimal
      numbers into binary and store the binary digits in B(I,J).

BIRD WATCHING CHART

BIRD	PLACE	WHEN	WHERE	SMALL	BIG	YELLOW	BLUE	SHORT-BEAKED	LONG-BEAKED	MALE	FEMALE
1	S	E	L	S		Y		S		M	
2	W	E	H	S		Y		S			F
3	D	E	L	S		Y			L	M	
4	F	E	H	S		Y			L		F
5	SW	M	L	S			B	S		M	
6	S D	M	H	S			B	S			F
7	S F	M	L	S			B		L	M	
8	WD	M	H	S			B		L		F
9	W F	ME	HL			Y		S		M	
10	DF	ME	HL		B	Y		S			F
11	WDF	ME	HL		B	Y			L	M	
12	S DF	ME	HL		B	Y			L		F
13	SW F	M	HL		B		B	S		M	
14	SWD	M	HL		B		B	S			F
15	SWDF	M	HL		B		B		L	M	
16	SWDF	M	HL		B		B		L		F

DIAMOND THIEF

Scenario

An expensive diamond is stolen from a museum. Your job, as the detective assigned to the case, is to determine who stole the diamond and at what time. You deduce the solution by studying the responses made by five different suspects, one of whom is guilty. Your rating is determined by how quickly you can identify the thief.

The five suspects were wandering through a nine room museum from one p.m. to twelve midnight. They never stayed in the same room for two consecutive hours, although they may have returned to the same room more than once.

You determine who you want to question and a specific time from one to twelve. The suspect responds by giving the following information:

1. Suspect's location at specified time
2. Whether or not the diamond was seen in room #5 at the specified time
3. Who was with the suspect
4. Who the suspect saw in adjacent rooms

There is a catch, however. The innocent suspects can forget the exact room they were in and may name adjacent rooms 5% of the time instead. There is also a 5% chance that innocent people will make errors in naming people in the room with them or people whom they saw. The thief makes errors 50% of the time. Any statement made about room #5 or any statement made about the diamond is always true.

The diamond was stolen at the end of the time interval; therefore, the thief or people in room #5 with the thief will claim to have seen the diamond during the time it was stolen. Of course, after the diamond was stolen, suspects will not have seen it.

When you think you know who the thief is and the time it was stolen, you should enter a zero in response to "suspect?". If you get either the thief or the time correct, you will get another chance, but will lose a ten question penalty on the final rating.

Sample Run

```
RUN
PLEASE WAIT
SOMEONE STOLE THE DIAMOND!!
QUESTION 1
SUSPECT (1-5)? 1
TIME? 6
SUSPECT 1 AT TIME 6
I WAS IN ROOM 8
I WAS WITH 3
I SAW 4

QUESTION 2
SUSPECT (1-5)? 4
TIME? 6
SUSPECT 4 AT TIME 6
I WAS IN ROOM 9
I SAW 1

QUESTION 3
SUSPECT (1-5)? 2
TIME? 6
I WAS IN ROOM 6
I SAW 4

QUESTION 4
SUSPECT (1-5)? 5
I WAS IN ROOM 1

QUESTION 5
SUSPECT (1-5)? 3
TIME? 7
I WAS IN ROOM 9
I WAS WITH 2
I SAW 4
  .
  .
  .
QUESTION 15
SUSPECT (1-5)? 4
TIME? 4
I WAS IN ROOM 5
I SAW THE DIAMOND
I WAS WITH 3

QUESTION 16
SUSPECT (1-5)? 0
GUILTY SUSPECT? 4
TIME OF CRIME? 4

YOU GOT "EM
THE THIEF IS 4 AT TIME 4.
YOUR RATING IS 84
PLAY AGAIN?
```

DIAMOND THIEF FLOWCHART

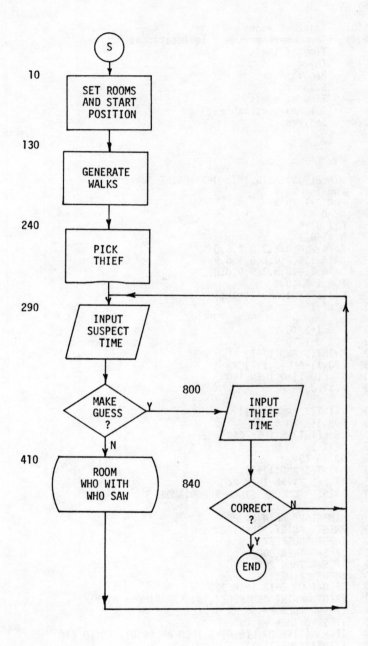

DIAMOND THIEF

Variables

A(I,J)	Adjacent rooms
L(I,J)	Room where person I is located at J time
T	Time of theft
D	Thief
P	Probability
S	Suspect
G	Time of guess
A	Temporary variable
I,J,K	Indices

Listing

```
10      DIM A(9,3), L(5,12): Q=1: PRINT "WAIT"
20      FOR I=1 TO 9
30      FOR J=1 TO 3
40      READ A
50      A(I,J)=A
60      NEXT J,I
70      DATA 2,4,0,1,3,0,2,6,0
80      DATA 1,5,7,4,6,8,3,5,9
90      DATA 4,8,0,5,7,9,6,8,0
100     FOR I=1 TO 5
110     L(I,1)=INT(RND(1)*9+1)
120     NEXT I

130     FOR I=2 TO 12
140     FOR J=1 TO 5
150     K=INT(3*RND(1)+1)
160     L(J,I)=A(L(J,I-1),K)
170     IF L(J,I)=0 THEN 150
180     NEXT J,I

190     T=INT(12*RND(1)+1)
200     FOR I=1 TO 5
210     IF L(I,T)=5 THEN 240
220     NEXT I
230     GO TO 190
240     D=INT(5*RND(1)+1)
250     IF L(D,T)<>5 THEN 240
260     PRINT "SOMEONE STOLE THE DIAMOND."

270     REM START MAIN LOOP
280     PRINT: PRINT "QUESTION"; Q
290     INPUT "SUSPECT"; S
300     IF S<1 THEN 800
310     IF S>5 THEN 290
320     INPUT "TIME"; G
330     IF G<1 OR G>12 THEN 320
340     PRINT: PRINT "SUSPECT"; S; "AT TIME"; G; ":"
350     IF S=D THEN P=.5
360     IF S<>D THEN P=.05
370     IF RND(1)>P OR L(5,6)=5 THEN A=L(S,G): GO TO 410
380     I=INT(3*RND(1)+1)
```

```
390    A=A(L(S,G),I)
400    IF A=0 OR A=5 THEN 380
410    PRINT: PRINT "I WAS IN ROOM"; A
420    IF A<>5 THEN 450
430    IF T<G THEN PRINT " I DID NOT SEE THE DIAMOND!": GO TO 450
440    PRINT "I SAW THE DIAMOND."
450    IF RND(1)<P THEN 510
460    FOR I=1 TO 5
470    IF I=S THEN 500
480    IF L(S,G)<>L(I,G) THEN 500
490    PRINT "I WAS WITH"; I
500    NEXT I: GO TO 540
510    I=INT(7*RND(1)+1): IF I=S THEN 510
520    IF I<6 THEN PRINT "I WAS WITH"; I
540    IF RND(1)<P THEN 640
550    FOR I=1 TO 3
560    A=A(L(S,G),I)
570    IF A=0 THEN 610
580    FOR J=1 TO 5
590    IF L(J,G)=A THEN PRINT "I SAW"; J
600    NEXT J
610    NEXT I
620    GO TO 700
640    J=INT(10*RND(1)+1)
650    IF J<5 THEN PRINT "I SAW"; J
700    IF RND(1)>P THEN 770
710    K=INT(10*RND(1)+1)
720    IF K<6 AND K<>J THEN PRINT "I SAW"; K
770    Q=Q+1: GO TO 280
800    INPUT "GUILTY SUSPECT"; S
810    IF S<1 OR S>5 THEN 800
820    INPUT "TIME OF CRIME"; G
830    IF G<1 OR G>12 THEN 820
840    IF S=D AND G=T THEN PRINT "YOU GOT 'EM!": GO TO 870
850    IF S=D OR G=T THEN PRINT "PARTLY RIGHT": Q=Q+10: GO TO 280
860    PRINT "BETTER GIVE UP": Q=Q+100
870    PRINT "THE THIEF IS"; D; "AT TIME"; T
900    PRINT "YOUR RATING IS"; 100-Q
910    INPUT "PLAY AGAIN"; Y$
920    IF Y$="Y" THEN RUN
930    END
```

DIAMOND THIEF MODIFICATIONS

Minor

1. Probability of thief lying -- line 350
2. Probability of innocent suspect lying -- line 360

Major

1. Change room design.
2. Have an accomplice.
3. Jewel is hidden after it is stolen.
4. A guard is roaming around the museum as well.
5. Give suspects and rooms actual names, for example, Mr. Smith is in the Red Room.

MUSEUM FLOOR PLAN

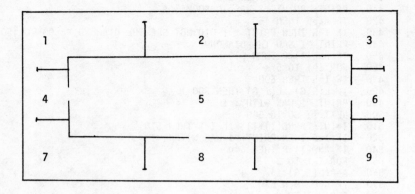

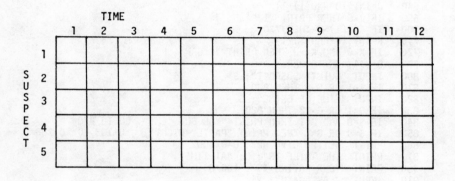

THE DEVIL'S DUNGEON

The Legend

For many years now you have heard rumors of large quantities of gold hidden in a maze of caves whose connecting passageways lead deep beneath the earth of an occasionally active volcano. The stories tell of monsters and demons who roam through the caves, poisonous gas, tremors from the volcano, and one man who returned from these perils alive and named the caves The Devil's Dungeon.

After much searching, you have located the wealthy, solitary man who survived a journey through the dungeon; and he has agreed to see you. Although now very old and in poor health, he tells you everything he can remember about the dungeon.

The Dungeon

There is much gold still remaining in this maze of caves called The Devil's Dungeon; and the stories of demons, monsters and poisonous gas are true. There are sixteen rooms on each level of the dungeon, although many may be blocked by rockfalls caused by volcanic tremors. The number of levels is unknown. Perhaps it is bottomless, for the creatures encountered inside the dungeon were certainly not from the earth as we know it.

Rooms and Passageways

You will begin your adventure in Room #1 at Depth #1. The contents of the room you occupy and the numbers of the adjacent rooms will be listed. You may move to an adjacent room by entering one of the adjacent room numbers. If the output reads: MOVE FROM 2 TO ?, all adjacent rooms on your present level are blocked. If a "slide" to a room is indicated, you may use it by entering that room number; however, it is a one-way passage and cannot be used to return to the first room. A simple map of connecting rooms at each depth will prove invaluable, even though you can receive a list of the rooms you have visited and their respective adjacent rooms any time you enter an 88.

Descending into the Dungeon

Movement to a lower depth can be achieved by using a dropoff. Fifty percent of the rooms at a given depth have dropoffs. To drop to a lower depth, enter any negative number when you are in one of these rooms. You will then find yourself in the same room on the next lower level. The configuration of rooms on this level will not be the same, and a new map must be drawn. Once you have left a given depth, you can never return. You cannot move up.

A dropoff can be created by using the Magic Wand, which you carry with you at all times. The use of the Magic Wand, however, is very risky, because 40% of the time it backfires. When a backfire occurs, your strength and speed are reduced by 50%. When the use of the wand is your only alternative, you must enter 99. If the wand works, it will clear out everything in the room and create a dropoff. If the wand backfires, you will remain in the same place with 50% of the strength and speed you had before using the wand. The Magic Wand can be used repeatedly in every room except Room #1. If you enter a 99 while in Room #1, the simulation will terminate.

Tremors

The contents and arrangements of rooms on each level remain the same throughout the journey. When you return to a room, everything will be the same, except, perhaps, the gold or monster. (See Gold and Monster.) The same passageways will be there leading to the same adjacent rooms, unless a tremor occurs. When a tremor occurs, some of the passageways may be blocked and others may be opened. To determine the effect of a tremor on passageways, you can enter an 88 to get a listing of open adjacent rooms to the rooms you have visited.

Room #1

Room #1 is very important on every level. It is the only room from which you may leave the dungeon by entering a 99. Room #1 is the only place at which you can increase your strength and speed. There are no hazards in this room. When you drop to a lower level, you will want to locate Room #1 as soon as possible.

Speed and Strength

Speed and strength are two qualities that must be maintained throughout your journey in order to survive. Both speed and strength are needed to kill a monster, but speed alone is needed to run from the monster. The curse of a demon affects your speed, and the poisonous gas affects your strength. You begin your journey with 100 units of both speed and strength. Each time you move to another room, your strength and speed will decrease by your depth. If you are at depth #4, the value of both your speed and strength will be decreased by 4 whenever you move. If at any time your strength or speed becomes zero or less, you are declared dead.

Experience

You begin with zero experience points. Everytime you move, your experience points are increased by your depth level number. You can also acquire up to the value of twice a monster's strength in experience points by killing the monster. One experience point is gained for every piece of gold found. Experience points can be traded for strength and speed, one for one, by entering a zero while in Room #1 at any depth. You will then be asked how many points you want added to your speed and to your strength.

Monsters

If a monster is present in a room, its speed and strength will be listed immediately after your speed and strength. If you elect to fight the monster, you must enter a zero. The monsters are faster and stronger in rooms with larger numbers and at lower depths. If your speed is faster than a monster's speed, you have a greater chance of attacking first. If your strength is greater, you have a better chance of killing it. If your speed and strength are two or three times that of the monsters', you will kill them most of the time. When you run from a monster instead of fighting it, speed is important. If a monster hits you on your way out of the room, you will lose 20% of the monster's strength. The monster cannot hit you if you use a dropoff or the Magic Wand in its room.

Demons and Poisonous Gas

About 25% of the rooms on each level have demons and about 25% of the rooms have poisonous gas Neither of these hazards can be eliminated, but you can escape from them. The demons and gas are always in these rooms and they should be avoided when possible. If you enter a room with demons or gas, there is a 40% chance that you will be cursed or gassed. If you are cursed, you will lose one-half of your strength. You can always escape being cursed or gassed by moving to a lower level.

Gold

The maximum amount of gold that could be in a room is stated when you enter the room. This quantity is directly related to the room number and depth. The amount of gold you actually find is given when you leave the room. This amount is a percentage of the maximum, randomly determined. You cannot take gold from a room unless you move to another room on the same level. Once you leave a room carrying gold, the gold is yours for the rest of the journey. Sometimes demons in the room with the gold will steal it as you leave. But whether you leave the room with the gold or demons steal it, when you return to that room, there will no longer be any gold there. You can take gold from a room only one time. If a monster is present in a room containing gold, you must kill the monster before you can take the gold. If you leave the room without killing the monster, the gold and the monster will remain in the room and be there when you return.

Summary

		Enter
In Room #1	to trade experience for strength and speed	0
	to end adventure	99
In any room except #1	to move to adjacent room on the same level	adjacent room #
	to fight monster	0
	to use a dropoff	any negative number
	to use Magic Wand	99
In any room	to list rooms visited	88

Sample Run

```
GOLD  0    EXP  0    DEPTH  1
YOUR SPEED  100    STRENGTH  100

SLIDE TO 2
MOVE FROM 1 TO 7?  7
```

```
GOLD  0    EXP  1    DEPTH  1
YOUR SPEED  99    STRENGTH  99

SLIDE TO 2
MOVE FROM 7 TO 1  2  6?  6
```

```
GOLD  0    EXP  2    DEPTH  1
YOUR SPEED  98    STRENGTH  98

MONSTER'S SPEED 6  STRENGTH 7
DROPOFF
MOVE FROM 6 TO 7  14?  14
```

```
ESCAPED
GOLD  0    EXP  3    DEPTH  1
YOUR SPEED  97    STRENGTH  97

MAXIMUM GOLD  57
MOVE 14 TO 6?  6
```

.
.
.

```
GOLD 25    EXP 31    DEPTH  1
YOUR SPEED  94    STRENGTH  5

MONSTER'S SPEED  8    STRENGTH 5
DEMONS
MAXIMUM GOLD  9
MOVE FROM 2 TO 5  7?  0
```

```
YOU ATTACK
MONSTER DEAD!
GOLD 25    EXP 41    DEPTH  1
YOUR SPEED  93    STRENGTH  91

DEMONS
MAXIMUM GOLD  9
MOVE FROM 2 TO 5  7?  5
```

```
YOU FOUND 6 PIECES OF GOLD
GOLD 31    EXP 48    DEPTH  1
YOUR SPEED  92    STRENGTH  90

MAXIMUM GOLD  21
MOVE FROM 5 TO 2  3  11?  11
```

.
.
.

```
GOLD 46    EXP 70    DEPTH  1
YOUR SPEED  84    STRENGTH  82

SLIDE TO 2
MOVE FROM 1 TO 7?  0
```

```
EXP 70    SPEED 84    STRENGTH  82
ADD SPEED?  34
EXP LEFT  36
ADD STRENGTH?  36
GOLD 46    EXP  0    DEPTH  1
YOUR SPEED  118    STRENGTH  118

SLIDE TO 2
MOVE FROM 1 TO 7?  7
```

.
.
.

MAP OF DEPTH 1
DRAWN BY PLAYER

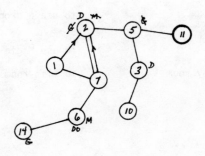

```
GOLD  46      EXP  2     DEPTH  1
YOUR SPEED 116      STRENGTH 116
MONSTER'S SPEED 6    STRENGTH 7

DROPOFF
MOVE FROM 6 TO 7  14?  -1
```

```
GOLD  46      EXP  2     DEPTH  2
YOUR SPEED 114      STRENGTH 114
MONSTER'S SPEED 14   STRENGTH 24

SLIDE TO 9
MOVE FROM 6 TO 2   4   12?   4
```

.
.
.

```
GOLD 179      EXP  2     DEPTH  2
YOUR SPEED 138      STRENGTH 137
MONSTER'S SPEED 30   STRENGTH 30

SLIDE TO 4
DROPOFF
MOVE FROM 11 TO 1?   -1
```

```
GOLD 179      EXP  2     DEPTH  3
YOUR SPEED  135     STRENGTH  134

POISONOUS GAS
SLIDE TO 6
MOVE FROM 11 TO 4   7   13?   7
```

```
GASSED
GOLD  179     EXP  5     DEPTH  3
YOUR SPEED  132     STRENGTH  64
MONSTER'S SPEED 42   STRENGTH 27

MOVE FROM 7 TO 2   6   11   13?   0
```

.
.
.

MAP OF DEPTH 2
DRAWN BY PLAYER

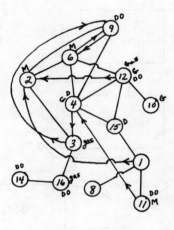

THE DEVIL'S DUNGEON FLOWCHART

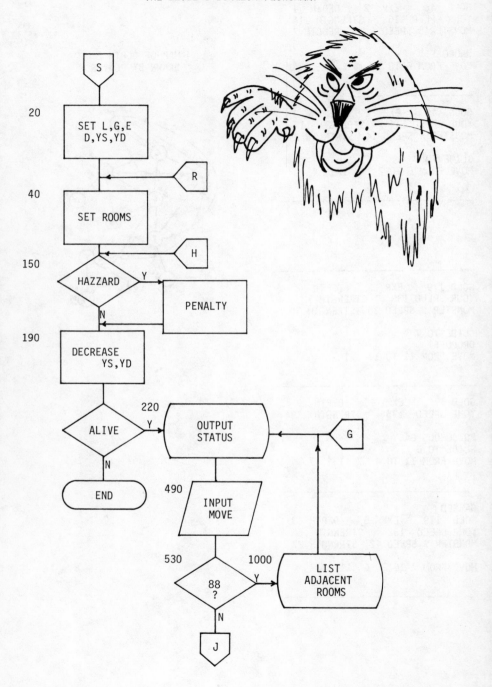

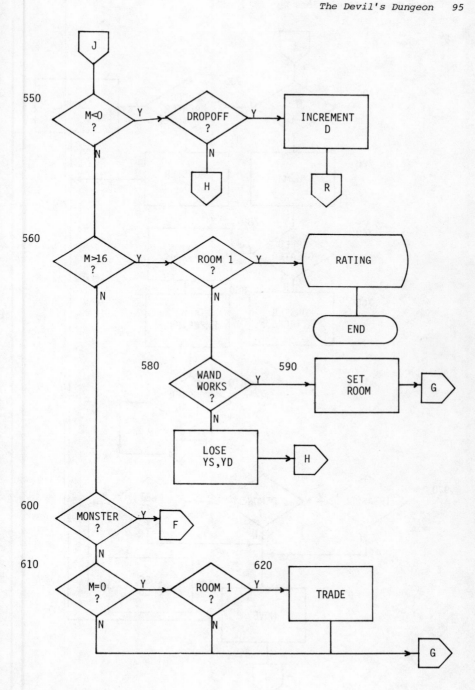

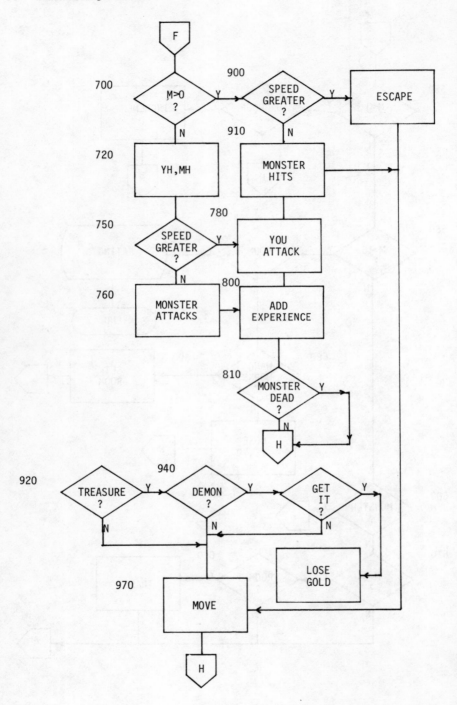

THE DEVIL'S DUNGEON PROGRAM

Variables

R(16)	0 - 524287	Specifies contents of room
L(65)	1 - 16	Lists adjacent rooms
F(16)	0 or 1	Set flags for adjacent rooms
X(19)	0 or 1	Flags for room contents (see below)
B(16)	0 or 1	Flags rooms already visited
L	1 - 16	Your location
G_1		Amount of gold in room -- depends on depth, size of room, and random factor
G		Total amount of gold that you have accumulated
E		Total experience points -- gained by moving, fighting, running, collecting gold -- can be traded for strength and speed
D	1 - ∞	Depth
YS		Your strength -- you die if it drops to 0
YD		Your speed -- you die if it drops to 0
YH		Your hit when fighting
MS		Monster's strength -- depends upon depth, size of room, and random factor
MD		Monster's speed
MH		Monster's hit when fighting
I,J		Indices
F	0 or 1	Flag for monster present
N,Q,R		Temporary variables
S		Slide
M		Move to
T		Treasure
S(1),X(12)		Demon
X(2)		Monster
S(3),X(4),X(5)		Monster's strength
X(6),X(7),X(8)		Monster's speed
X(9),X(11)		Poisonous gas
X(10)		Treasure
S(14)		Slide
X(15) - X(18)		Slide to room
X(19)		Dropoff
X		Number of rooms

Listing

```
  5   REM SET ROOMS
 10   DIM R(16),L(65),F(16),X(19),B(16)
 20   L=1: G=Ø: E=Ø: X=16
 30   D=1: YS=1Ø1: YD=1Ø1
 40   FOR I=Ø TO 65: L(I)=Ø :NEXT
 50   FOR I=1 TO X: N=INT(3*RND(1)+1)
 60   IF I=1 THEN N=3
 70   FOR J=1 TO N
 80   R=INT(64*RND(1)+1)
 90   IF L(R)<>Ø THEN 8Ø
100   L(R)=I
110   NEXT J
120   R(I)=INT(524287*RND(1)):B(I)=Ø
130   NEXT I:B(L)=1
```

```
140   R(1)=24576:FOR I=1 TO 19:X(I)=∅:NEXT

145   REM HAZARDS
150   IF RND(1)<.∅1 THEN PRINT "TREMOR":FOR I=1 TO 2∅:L(I)=
      INT(X*RND(1)+1):NEXT
160   IF RND(1)<.∅1 THEN PRINT "TREMOR":FOR I=1 TO 2∅:L(I)=∅:NEXT
170   IF X(1)*X(12)=1 AND RND(1)<.4 THEN PRINT "CURSED BY DEMON!":
      YD=INT(.5*YD)
180   IF X(9)*X(11)=1 AND RND(1)<.4 THEN PRINT "GASSED!":YS=
      INT(.5*YS)

185   REM DECREMENT AND TEST
190   YD=YD-D
200   YS=YS-D
210   IF YS<=∅ OR YD<=∅ THEN PRINT "YOU'RE DEAD":END

215   REM OUTPUT STATUS
220   PRINT "GOLD"; G; "      ";
230   PRINT "EXP."; E; "DEPTH"; D
240   PRINT "SPEED:    ";YD; "STRENGTH:    ";YS:GOSUB 25∅:GOTO31∅

245   REM ADJACENT ROOMS
250   FOR I=1 TO X: F(I)=∅:NEXT
260   FOR I=1 TO 64
270   IF L<>L(I) THEN3∅∅
280   IF L(I+1)<>∅ AND L(I+1)<>L THEN F(L(I+1))=1
290   IF L(I-1)<>∅ AND L(I-1)<>L THEN F(L(I-1))=1
300   NEXT:RETURN

305   REM CONVERT
310   N=R(L)
320   FOR I=1 TO 19:Q=INT(N/2):X(I)=2*(N/2-Q):N=Q:NEXT

325   REM MONSTERS, DEMONS, GAS
330   IF X(2)=∅ THEN MS=∅:GOTO38∅
340   IF F=1 THEN 37∅
350   MS=D*(X(3)+2*X(4)+4*X(5)+L)
360   MD=D*(X(6)+2*X(7)+4*X(8)+L)
370   PRINT "MONSTER'S SPEED:";MD;"STRENGTH:";MS
380   IF X(1)*X(12)=1 THEN PRINT "DEMONS"
390   IF X(9)*X(11)=1 THEN PRINT "POISONOUS GAS"

395   REM TREASURE
400   IF X(1∅)<>1 THEN T=∅:GOTO43∅
410   T=X(11)+2*X(12)+4*X(13)+1
420   PRINT"MAXIMUM GOLD:";T*L*D+1

425   REM SLIDES AND DROPOFFS
430   S=X(15)+2*X(16)+4*X(17)+8*X(18)+1
440   IF S>X THEN S=1
450   IF S=∅ THEN S=1
460   IF X(14)=∅ OR S=L THEN48∅
470   PRINT "SLIDE TO:";S
480   IF X(19)*X(13)=1 THEN PRINT"DROPOFF"

485   REM INPUT MOVE
490   PRINT"MOVE FROM";L;"TO";
500   FOR I=1 TO X
510   IF F(I)=1 AND I<>L THEN PRINT I;
520   NEXT I
```

```
530     INPUT M:IF M=88 THEN1000
540     IF M<0 AND X(19)*X(13)=1 THEN D=D+1:F=0:GOTO40
550     IF M<0 THEN PRINT"NO DROPOFF":GOTO 150
560     IF M>X AND L=1 THEN PRINT"YOU FOUND";G;"PIECES OF GOLD.":END
570     IF M<X THEN600

575     REM MAGIC WAND
580     IF RND(1)<.4 THENPRINT"BACKFIRE":YS=INT(.5*YS):YD=INT(.5*YD):
        GOTO150
590     PRINT"WAND WORKS":R(L)=266240:GOTO220

595     REM MOVE TRADE
600     IF MS>0 THEN700
610     IF M<>0 OR L<>1 THEN920
620     PRINT"EXPERIENCE";E;"SPEED";YD;"STRENGTH";YS:INPUT"ADD SPEED";N
630     IF E-N<0 THEN PRINT"NEED MORE EXPERIENCE":GOTO620
640     E=E-N:YD=YD+N:PRINT"EXPERIENCE LEFT";E
650     INPUT"ADD STRENGTH";N
660     IF E-N<0 THEN PRINT"NEED MORE EXPERIENCE":GOTO650
670     E=E-N:YS=YS+N
680     GOTO220

695     REM FIGHT
700     F=1
710     IF M>0 THEN900
720     YH=INT(RND(1)*YS):MH=INT(RND(1)*MS)
730     IF YH>MS THEN YH=MS
740     IF MH>YS THEN MH=YS
750     IF RND(1)*YD>RND(1)*MD THEN 780
760     PRINT"MONSTER ATTACKS":YS=YS-MH:MS=MS-INT(.5*YH)
770     GOTO800
780     PRINT"YOU ATTACK":MS=MS-YH:YS=YS-INT(.5*MH)
800     E=E+2*YH
810     IF MS<=0 THEN PRINT"MONSTER DEAD!":R(L)=R(L)-2:GOTO150
815     PRINT
820     PRINT"MONSTER STILL ALIVE":GOTO150

895     REM RUN
900     IF RND(1)*YD>RND(1)*MD THEN PRINT"ESCAPED":GOTO970
910     PRINT"MONSTER HIT YOU":YS=YS-INT(.2*MS):GOTO970

915     REM TREASURE
920     IF T=0 THEN970
930     G1=INT(RND(1)*T*L*D)+1
940     IF X(1)*X(12)=1 AND RND(1)<.4 THEN PRINT"DEMON GOT GOLD!":G1=0
950     PRINT"YOU FOUND";G1;"PIECES OF GOLD.":G=G+G1:R(L)=R(L)-512
960     E=E+G1

965     REM MOVE
970     IF F(M)=1 OR M=S THEN L=M:F=0:E=E+D:B(L)=1:GOTO150
980     PRINT"NOT ADJACENT":GOTO150

995     REM PRINT ROOMS
1000    L1=L:FOR K=1 TO X
1010    IF B(K)<>1 THEN1070
1020    PRINT K; "--";
1030    L=K:GOSUB250
1040    FOR J=1 TO X
1050    IF F(J)=1 AND J<>K THEN PRINT J;
```

```
1060    NEXT J:PRINT
1070    NEXT K
1080    L=L1:GOTO220
```

THE DEVIL'S DUNGEON MODIFICATIONS

Minor

1. To change initial amount of gold or initial amount of experience, change the appropriate variable in line 20.
2. To begin at a lower level, increase D in line 30.
3. To begin with a different amount of strength or speed, change YS and/or YD in line 30.
4. To increase the probability of a tremor, increase .01 in line 150 and/or line 160.
5. To increase the probability of being cursed by a demon/gassed, increase the .4 in line 170.
6. To increase the effect of being cursed/gassed, decrease the .5 in line 170/180.
7. To double the monster's strength/speed, insert a statement, MS=2*MS/MD=2*MD at line 355/365.
8. To increase the probability of demons/gas in a room from 25% to 50%, remove the X(12)/X(11) from lines 170/180 and 380/390.
9. To double the treasure, insert the statement, T=2*T in line 415.
10. To increase the probability of a dropoff in a room from 25% to 50%, remove the X(13) from lines 480 and 540.
11. To increase the probability of the wand backfiring, increase the .4 in line 580.
12. To increase the effect of the wand backfiring, decrease the .5 in line 580.
13. To increase the amount the monster loses/you lose when attacking, increase the .5 in line 760/780.
14. To increase the amount of experience you gain while fighting, increase the 2 in line 800.
15. To increase the amount you lose when getting hit while running from the monster, increase the .2 in line 910.

Major

1. Weapons and equipment must be bought with gold before starting on the journey.
2. There could be different sized monsters, determined by the expression, X(3)+2*X(4)+4*X(5) in line 350. Each monster could be named, ie, Glub, Knaw, Slurp, Hairy, ...
3. The treasures could be in various sized containers, determined by the expression, X(11)+2*X(12)+4*X(13) in line 410.
4. The number of rooms at each level could be determined randomly.
5. Some rooms could be light and others dark.
6. Some monsters or demons could appear at random rather than be assigned to specific rooms.
7. A mean magician could relocate you in another room.
8. You could accidentally fall into a pit that drops you to a lower level.